STEPS OF CORE
CORE 4 DO MO

FEW TIPS:
IN YOUR
CORE R
JOR FUNCTION
SL
LAW ON THE WWDB WEB
OR EACH 90 DAY CORE RUN
SEND COPY TO YOUR

STEPS OF CORE

THEMSELVES TO
FREE
IF YOU STOP AND THINK ABOUT IT EVERY
THAT IS MAN MADE THAT YOU WAS 1st JUST
IN SOMEONE'S IMAGINATION.

MOTIV
OUR FU
ALL AN IMAGINA

MAKE OUR OWN C
IT IS EASY TO DO EASY NOT

THAT IS WHY IT'S SO IMPORTANT THAT YOU US
YOUR IMAGINATION TO DREAM OF WHAT YOU W
YOUR FUTURE TO LOOK LIKE 1st. TO WRITE IT D
TAKE PICTURES OF IT AND PUT IT ON YOUR REFRIG
OR BATHROOM MIRROR SO YOU SEE IT EVERY DAY.
OPPO
ON HOW
FR
VISION IS THE DRIVE IN YOUR LIFE IT
IS WHAT WILL KEEP YOU DRIVING TOWARDS YOUR
GOAL AND NOT QUIT ON YOURSELF. WITHOUT A
VISION YOU WILL BE MOVED BY A CLOCK (TIME)
A DREAM WITHOUT ACTION IS A HALLUCINATION
A DREAM WITH ACTION BECOMES A VISION.
YOUR DREAMS + GOALS WILL CHANGE AS
YOU PROGRESS TOWARDS YOUR VISION BUT YOUR
VISION + PURPOSE FOR YOUR LIFE WILL REMAIN
THE SAME.
YOUR DREAMS AND GOALS WILL MOTIVATE,
ENCOURAGE + REWARD YOU AS YOU PURSUE
YOUR LIFE LONG PURPOSE AND VISION FOR YOUR
LIFE.

BUSIN
1. - WWDB - DEBT FREE - AND
2. - MANAGEMENT TEAM (RO TOP DIAMON
70% VOTE REQUIRED TO CHANGE OUR CULTURE
3. - APPROVED SYSTEM BY AMWAY CORP. WE NEVE
BREAK AMWAY'S RULES, GOD'S LAWS OR M
LAWS.
4. - VERTICAL ALIGNMENT - PRIORITIES
A - GOD - PAUL + BILLIE TSIKA
B - SPOUSE / CHILDREN

AMWAY - THE VEHICLE
WHAT MAKES IT SO SPECIAL?
1 - FOUNDED BY 2 CHRISTIAN MEN AND
   - THE SALES + MKTG. PLAN WAS DESIGNED
     ON GOD'S LAWS OF SUCCESS - BEING A GIVER
     INSTEAD OF TAKER - LAW OF SOWING
     AND REAPING (WILL EXPLAIN TOMORROW AFTERNOON)
     (~~COMPASSIONATE CAPITALISM~~)

2 - PRIVATE CORPORATION - (CONTROL) OF The
   MKTG. PLAN - KEEP IT PURE)

3 - DEBT FREE (AWESOME POWER IN
   COMPETITIVE GLOBAL MARKET) - 45
   COUNTRIES + TERRITORYS)

4 - 5000 + PRODUCTS + SERVICES - BRAND
   NAMES

AND EMOTION-DRIVEN
RACTER-DRIVEN PEOPLE:
DO RIGHT, THEN FEEL GOOD
ARE COMMITMENT DRIVEN
MAKE PRINCIPLE-BASED DECISIONS
4. LET ACTION
5. BELIEVE IT
6. CREATE MO
7. ASK, "WHA
8. CONTINUE
9. ARE STI
10. ARE LE

THINK IT
JUST ONE
DISCIPLINE, DECIS
FINISH, THAT'S
THAT DRIVE US T
ERS

(7)

IGNORANCE (INDEEDS)
FAMILY PROBLEMS (HUS + WIFE)
FINANCIAL PROBLEMS (BUDGET)
JOB PROBLEMS
PEOPLE SKILLS

E.D.C.

DIAMOND

EMERALD

RUBY

D.D.

INCOME D.
HAR
COR

1YR   2YR   3YR   4YR

A
DREAM → VISION
FAITH → B
CORE → BELIEF ADDS

12 | PRINCIPLES THAT BUILT
WORLD WIDE DREAMBUILDERS

TRUE
NORTH

GEORGIA LEE PURYEAR

LIBERTY LAKE, WASHINGTON

For more information, contact
GB & G Foundation
P.O. Box 972
Liberty Lake, Washington 99019

Manuscript prepared by Rick and Melissa Killian,
Killian Creative, Boulder, Colorado
www.killiancreative.com

Front cover photo of Ron Puryear by Brian Gavriloff.
Author photo by Alicia Puryear.
Design by Peter Gloege, LOOK Design Studio

ISBN: 978-1-7345257-0-0

Printed in the United States of America
21 22 23 24 25 26 27 28 29 30 (LBM) 10 9 8 7 6 5 4 3 2 1

This book is dedicated first and foremost to
the Lord.
Thank you for always showing us the path.

Secondly, this book is dedicated to
the love of my life, Ron.
Thank you for always being faithful
to keeping us on the path.

Lastly, this book is dedicated to all of
World Wide Dreambuilders.
May we always stay on the path.

I Love You More,
Georgia Lee

CONTENTS

"Why World Wide Works" by John C. Maxwell ix

"Among God's Giants" by Paul E. Tsika xiii

Acknowledgments xvii

Introduction: The Path of True North... xix

1   It's About Where You're Going More Than Where You've Been 3

2   Don't Let Anything Steal Your Dream 15

3   Turning Your Dream into a Vision 35

4   Growing Goal by Goal 53

5   You Need to Live for Something Greater Than Yourself 69

6   It's a Business, Not a J-O-B 83

7   The Second Mountain 99

8   Wisdom Comes from Experience 115

9   Outer Success Is Built from Inner Character 131

10 You Will Reap What You Sow—*Multiplied* 145

11 All That Glitters 165

12 Why We Use Family Language 177

The Twelve Principles 184

Appendix A: "The Ideal Business" by Ron Puryear 187

Appendix B: The Ten CORE Habits for Success 199

Notes 203

Author Bio 204

Why World Wide Works

I just finished reading *True North: 12 Principles that Built World Wide Dreambuilders*. I'm so glad I did! My respect for Ron and Georgia Lee Puryear has always been at the core of our relationship. For the past fifteen years, I have known that they are the "Real Deal." However, reading about their early years of marriage and business drew me even closer to them.

Often, I teach that everything worthwhile is uphill. Ron and Georgia Lee's journey has been uphill *all* the way! Their road to success was uphill and rocky. Lack of parental support in the business . . . now that's a big rock to climb over! Needing Georgia Lee's tip money from Denny's to make ends meet . . . will that rock ever go away? Ron throwing up before he made his early presentations . . . that's a rock that needs to be moved every week!

This book is a must read for anyone considering becoming a part of the World Wide family. As you turn the pages, you will realize that blood, sweat, and tears gave birth to this organization. An unlikely couple in an unlikely place with unlikely odds accomplished an unlikely dream! They did it—and you can too!

WHY WORLD WIDE WORKS

Allow me to pull out the "secret sauce" of why World Wide Dreambuilders is a successful organization. Be proud! What can be said of the Puryears can be said about you.

Values: When people learn and live good values, they become more valuable to themselves and others. Practically every page expresses a positive value that should be the foundation of your family and business.

Wisdom: The principles lived by Ron and Georgia Lee, and the Diamonds of World Wide, were birthed out of adversity. They have been tested and proven to help you on your business journey.

Hope: The leaders of World Wide are dealers in hope. Hope is more than positive thinking. Hope is a result of positive doing! This business will give you exactly what you work for. The dream is free, but the journey isn't.

Opportunity: My friend Chuck Swindoll says, "We are all faced with a series of great opportunities brilliantly disguised as impossible situations." Ron and Georgia Lee continually faced "impossible situations." They got through the problems so they could get to the opportunities.

Tenacity: Ron and Georgia Lee greatly admire Margaret

Thatcher, the "Iron Lady," who was prime minister of England. She said, "You may have to fight a battle more than once to win it." How true! Perseverance, tenacity, and determination are essential to succeed in this business. The Diamonds of World Wide have carried on that spirit of their founders.

Family: Family values have been the core of World Wide Dreambuilders from the beginning. Strong individual families make a strong organization. Family first has given you a backbone, not a wishbone. Success is having those who know you the best love and respect you the most. That is the culture of their business.

Faith: Hope is not easily defined, but it is impossible to embrace without faith. Ron and Georgia Lee have modeled faith-based living for the organization since the very beginning. I remember well when Ron and I spent an afternoon together talking about his heart for God. He asked me to speak on Sundays at the Spring Leadership conference. Thousands have received Christ in those services. It is one of the highlights of my life.

This book closes with a presentation from Ron at the 2012 Leadership event. His talk was entitled, "The Ideal Business." His thesis was, "Amway, more than any other business, is the 'Ideal Business.'" He gave eleven characteristics of an ideal business. Please read it . . . it's powerful!

He closed his speech with typical Ron Puryear humility. Here's what he said:

If Georgia Lee and I can do it, you can do it. You've heard our story. We're nothing special. We're just very ordinary people who were in deep trouble in every area of our life, and we were fortunate to have somebody care enough about us to share this business with us—this unique and special business. We didn't know how unique and special it was at first, but I knew one thing: It was something I could do. I could fit that in somewhere in my week.

Why? Because I had a dream big enough to make me want more for my family. That dream caused me to start the process and never quit. I just stayed consistent through the good times, the bad times, the frustrating times, and the disappointing times. That's life. That's part of any business—and if you're going to go through that anyway, why not do it while building something for yourself and your family? I knew what the rewards were, and I kept after them.

What about you? What's your dream? How far will it take you? I think it's time to find out.

John C. Maxwell
Author of *Developing the Leader Within You*
and more than one hundred other books

Among God's Giants

All God's giants have been weak men [and women],
who did great things for God because they reckoned
on His being with them.

—HUDSON TAYLOR
British missionary giant (1832–1905)

When I think of Ron and Georgia Lee Puryear, I'm reminded that Paul the Apostle said that only in his weakness could he find his strength in Christ. (See 2 Corinthians 12:10.)

That's the conclusion you will hopefully come to as you read *True North*. Georgia Lee exposes, in a most gracious and honest way, their journey. She shares their struggles, weaknesses, doubts, and fears, but through it all, the unfailing faithfulness of God.

I was privileged, like many of the Diamonds in the World Wide Group, to have had a close personal relationship with Ron and Georgia

Lee. As I read her book, I laughed, wept, and read things I did not know about their journey.

I was captivated as Georgia Lee shared from her heart with open, honest transparency and with a willingness to laugh at their circumstances.

To countless thousands of people, they are considered heroes. But they never thought of themselves in that way.

Christopher Reeve said, "A hero is an ordinary individual who finds the strength to persevere and endure in spite of overwhelming obstacles." And who would know better than Superman?

That definition of hero fits Ron and Georgia Lee perfectly.

> *Ron and Georgia Lee have always been strong, determined, and very focused. But at the same time, they have an extremely tender heart for everyone.*

Ron and Georgia Lee have always been strong, determined, and very focused. But at the same time, they have an extremely tender heart for everyone. The thought of ever hurting anyone with their words or actions is the last thing they'd ever want.

When I first came on board as the pastor/advisor to WWDB, my wife, Billie Kaye, and I had a meeting with Ron and Georgia Lee. I can remember that meeting in 2000 like it was yesterday. We sat in that restaurant near the River House.

Ron said, "Paul and Billie, Georgia Lee and I are in total agreement that we can accomplish anything God puts before us, as long we don't care who gets the credit, people get the help they need, and God gets the glory."

That defines Ron and Georgia Lee Puryear and their belief of how a dreambuilder builds their dream.

Ron and Georgia Lee have always loved, appreciated, and greatly valued their Diamond leaders. They have never been about a lot of public praise, but I can assure you they know this book would not be possible without those leaders and their love for them.

As one man has said, "What's the first thing you know when you see a turtle sitting on a fence post? Someone else put him there."

That "someone else" was the Diamond leaders in WWDB. I know personally how much Ron and Georgia Lee counted on their love and their wisdom to carry on the legacy in World Wide that they birthed.

Which is exactly what's happening as I type.

This is a remarkable book filled with remarkable stories about a remarkable couple and their dream.

Enjoy!

Paul E. Tsika
Pastor/Advisor WWDB

Acknowledgments

This book would never have been written and completed without the help and loving guidance of my daughter-in-law Bobbie, my son Jim, and my sister, Kathy. For each of you, I am forever grateful.

I want to thank all of the WWDB Diamonds:

Theron & Darlene Nelsen	Ryder & Nicole Erickson
Terry & Linda Felber	David & Jaimee Felber
Bill & Sandy Hawkins	Leif & Bonnie Johnson
Dave & Jan Severn	Ross & Leslie Hall
Jim & Judy Head	Greg & Laurie Duncan
Steve & Chris Cummins	Gator & Connie Strong
Toshi & Bea Taba	Al & Kathy Gallo
Ken & Gail Stokes	Terry & Fran Woodhead
Bill & Nancy Kelly	Gene & Sheryl Lamazor
Roger & Joyce Fix	Brad & Julie Duncan
Joe & Norma Foglio	Norm & Pam Kizirian
Dave & Darlene Duncan	Debbie Shores
Jeff & Leslie Rice	Dan & Sandy Yuen
Dave & Mary Timko	Rod & Penny Alcott
Glen & Joya Baker	Scott & Cris Harimoto
Matt & Sandee Tsuruda	Frank & Lynn Radford
Mike & Michi Woods	Randy & Sandy Sears
Greg & Kathy Gilmour	Mike & Robin Carroll
Howie & Theresa Danzik	Hal & Ann Golden
Larry & Julie Koning	Rick & Bonnie Marshall

Gary & Dorothy Lowary

Dayne & Ivanette Kaneshiro

Bob & Shelly Kummer

Nam-Deuk Kim & Jungyun Lee

Tracey & Kimberly Eaton

Francis Cho & Hyunkyung Kim

Ty & Venessa Crandell

Ryan & Noella Olynyk

Mandy Yamamoto

Randy & Raye-Lynn Jassman

Jon & Jen Rosario

Shane and Joey Yadao

Kelly and Darci Ewing

Samir & Theresa Attalah

Ed & Karen Grosboll

Tom & Valerie Gonser

Sunki Kim & Misun Yoon

Jay & Jeong Lee

Dean & Marcie Whalen

Trevor & Lexi Baker

Pete & Rachael Herschelman

Terry & Jenny Brown

Matt & Briley Nguyen

Kevin and Andrea Phillips

Kenny and Ashlea Toms

Thank you for all of your respect and support of Ron and the responsibility God placed on him. To list every story would have been beyond the scope of this book and taken several volumes. Know that I hold every experience I have had with each of you in my heart and I am thankful to God for having you in my life. You are all blessings to me.

Thank you, Paul and Billie Kaye Tsika, for your continual spiritual guidance and care that you sow into all of WWDB. God's plan is perfect. And thank you, Paul, for being an incredible friend to Ron.

Thank you, John Maxwell, for taking time from your busy, busy life to send messages of encouragement to Ron. Your words of wisdom were gems, and your humor and jokes were joy.

I also want to thank all of the WWDB staff. Your willingness to serve the whole organization does not go unnoticed. Ron was so appreciative of you and proud of you. You are the best.

Georgia Lee

Introduction:
The Path of True North

Then I saw that there is more gain in wisdom than in folly,
as there is more gain in light than in darkness.

—KING SOLOMON[1]

When Ron and I became Amway Independent Business Owners in 1971 (well, Ron did in 1971; I didn't get on board until the next year), we didn't imagine where God would lead us in the years to come. We had no idea of the lessons we'd learn, the personal and professional growth we would experience, the battles we would fight, the triumphs and struggles we would face, or the joys we would experience as the family of World Wide Dreambuilders came into existence and grew into what it is today: one of the world's largest and fastest-growing IBO support systems. World Wide has been around for more than forty years, and I still remember its foundational meeting in Sunriver, Oregon.

But I am not here to tell WWDB tales or to honor Ron, as much as I love and miss him every day. There is simply not enough space here to tell about all of the wonderful adventures we have shared with the Diamonds in World Wide. That would require several books and, while fun and interesting, it wouldn't increase our story's impact. I don't have the space to tell each and every Diamond, past and present (more than 60 now), how I feel about you. Please know that I love and respect each and every one of you for who you are, what you have accomplished, and the love you have given our family. I don't like talking about myself, and I don't want to pretend that Ron and I are more special than anyone else. We're not special; we are small-town folk who got the chance to chase down some of our dreams, and we learned a lot in the process.

This brings me to the reason I wrote this book: You need to know why WW is the way it is, so you can build on what we did and do something better for yourself. I want you to see what we did, avoid our failures, and embrace the principles we found tried and true, because they will help you achieve your dreams. I hope this book will be a bedrock for the *next* forty years. I want you to understand what went into making World Wide what it is today, so you can build on that foundation to make it even better in the years to come.

This is important, because the principles that built World Wide are not anything new. Integrity, honor, determination, and love will never go out of style. For centuries, human beings have tried to find a better way, and we have made some improvements in lifestyle and technical know-how, but the people-to-people qualities that create family and make life worth living have endured for thousands of years. The keys to building a business that is a network of valued relationships (and a business that helps people realize their dreams) remain unchanged. Yes, people have differing perspectives and personalities, but north will always be north.

That's a good thing, because it helps us get from where we are now to where we want to go.

I want to share with you what Ron and I found to be true so that you can surpass our accomplishments. I want you to get from where you are now to where you want to go, and beyond. For this, you'll need to understand an idea Ron taught faithfully, an idea still central to being a success in this business. He asserted that we must navigate our life and business according to True North.

> *Yes, people have differing perspectives and personalities, but north will always be north.*

What does this look like? Imagine you have a dream, and the journey toward that dream is like going to the North Pole. You are going to need some things to guide you along, to ensure you stay on track. A compass, perhaps? Unfortunately, a compass will take you only so far before it becomes useless.

Why? A compass relies on magnetism to determine north, and, as you probably know, the magnetic North Pole is not the same as the actual North Pole. In fact, the magnetic North Pole moves, traveling approximately thirty-five miles a year. In 2005 it was in the Canadian Arctic Region. As you read these words, it's probably about 250 miles south of the geographic North Pole, in the direction of Seattle. That moving mass is helpful the farther south you are, but the closer you get to your dream of being at the North Pole, the farther off course it will take you.

At times, the geographic North Pole and the magnetic North Pole are more than 600 miles apart.

Because of this, if you're standing virtually anywhere in the United States, your compass will point north correctly enough for you to navigate from one location to another (with standard "magnetic declinations," as anyone who's navigated by compass knows). By simply glancing at your compass, you can get a general feel for how to go west to the Pacific Ocean or east to the Atlantic Ocean. However, if you're traipsing through the wilderness on a long hike, trying to hit something as small as a water source with your compass, and you don't correctly adjust for that area's magnetic declination, you could end up miles away from where you want to go.

> *A compass is like your personality and ingenuity, while the sextant represents long-established wisdom. In the beginning, your personality and drive are extremely helpful because they are motivating forces. . . . However, your personality and ideas will eventually give you false readings.*

Further, if your goal is to reach the North Pole, eventually your compass will start to lead you astray. It will take you to the magnetic North Pole, not the true North Pole.

To get to the true North Pole, a sextant is more valuable than a compass, because it helps you determine where you are in relation to the sun's position in the sky. That position is far more regular and predictable. If you know the date and the time, you can calculate the sun's position. Then you will be able to calculate your coordinates, your desired direction, and your distance from that destination.

So, if the true North Pole is your destination, a compass is like your personality and ingenuity, while the sextant represents long-established wisdom. In the beginning, your personality and drive are extremely helpful because they are motivating forces. They get you moving and headed roughly in the right direction.

However, your personality and ideas will eventually give you false readings. Because your perspective is limited and this is a trip you've never made, you will get something wrong. That's what happened to Ron and me. Your own thoughts will tell you such-and-such is the correct course to your goal, but the truth is you are off-target. Your opinions and assumptions will take you in the wrong direction. That is bad enough for you, but if you are leading others when you are off-course, so are they.

The good news is that others have made this trip before. They have a reliable road map to get you to where they have been—and where you want to go. They have a sextant they can loan you and teach you how to use. They have wisdom that is time-tested and proven effective. This wisdom will let you monitor your progress toward achieving your dreams, and it will keep you on course. You can still add your own touches and flourishes, of course. You get to pack your own suitcase. But you'll want to use that reliable road map rather than inventing one as you travel.

Please don't misunderstand me: This is not about your doing things "the company way." It's not an attempt to put you into a box. Those sharing their wisdom with you aren't trying to tell you what to do. They are telling you how they made their journey. They are merely providing principles that are like sextant readings to direct your path. They will also share how they went astray when they followed their own ideas. They will tell you how valuable it was to have an experienced person get them back on track. That person gave them principles, and those principles turned out to be the correct directions to the destination. Once they knew that these principles worked, they shared them with others they wanted to help. Over time, those principles were honed, becoming more universal and easier to follow.

The story of the Donner Party comes to mind. They had a trail guide to California. They had good information from an experienced trail boss. But they chose to ignore the trail boss's advice and tried a shortcut that was recommended in a guidebook written by a lawyer named Lansford Hastings. (Unfortunately, Hastings had never trekked the entire shortcut himself, and not in winter.)

The party, led by George Donner, ended up stuck in the mountains through the winter, with no food. Some who survived resorted to cannibalism.

—Jim Puryear

This is what True North is all about—giving you the Dreambuilder's accurate road map and the best advice. It's about the principles we used to build our business and establish World Wide Dreambuilders. It's about the events that helped us find True North.

Over the years, even before World Wide existed, God was teaching Ron and me what we needed to do to build our business and help others do the same. That is where the idea of being CORE came from—of following the Ten CORE Habits so that your business will grow. During those early years, we developed the Five Cardinal Rules so we could make sure we were always operating ethically. It is why Ron gave World Wide to the Diamonds and why the Management Team was formed. It is also why World Wide operates the way she does today, to keep all of her IBOs vibrant and growing.

These are the principles I want to share with you in this book. I want you to understand where they came from, so you can stay True North as you pursue your dreams. Thousands of years ago, King Solomon wrote expansively on wisdom and its timelessness. It's human nature to adjust and modify what we learn to make it more personal, but that's not the way of wisdom. One of the greatest struggles anyone faces in building their own business is knowing when to do things differently and when to stick to tradition. We need to take constant sextant readings to make sure we are on course. We need to be constantly realigning our voyage according to True North principles. When we do, our trip is always faster and easier.

> *One of the greatest struggles anyone faces in building their own business is knowing when to do things differently and when to stick to tradition.*

Ron saw the need to stay True North as he was building our business and helping others build theirs. He saw that if folks didn't make constant course corrections and know these wisdom principles thoroughly, it would affect the growth of their businesses. That's tricky, because magnetic north can look a whole lot like True North at times, but they are different, especially the closer you get to your dream. That is why, now, a few years after Ron has gone home to be with the Lord, it's time to revisit the principles that make World Wide great and see how we will use them to navigate the next forty years. There is still so much potential to be realized.

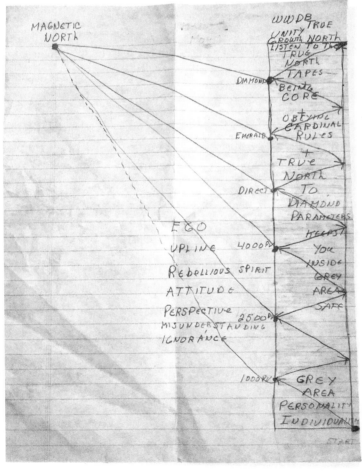

These were Ron's orginal notes
on his True North teaching.

Owning your business as an IBO will give you wings, and being part of World Wide will give you roots. Roots give us the stability we need while we grow. They anchor us as we learn, as we change, and they give us a place to return to and begin anew when we fail. The roots of World Wide are buried deeply, very deeply, in the love, respect, and friendship we had with Bill and Peggy Britt, with all the Diamonds who are World Wide, and with every World Wide member today.

> " *I pray that each of you has a "hang in there" attitude—that you will be able to hang in, hang on, hang out, hang loose, but never hang it up.* "

While roots give us stability and feed us from deep within, wings enable us to rise to our potential and realize our dreams. The Lord blessed Ron and me with a "hang in there" attitude. Many times, our wings grew weary and we feared we were going to nose-dive, but our attitude kept us going, kept us doing, and kept us achieving. Our attitude kept us growing and climbing. It allowed us to make our wings stronger so we could fly higher and be free. It gave us patience to idle our motors when all we really wanted to do was strip our gears. It gave us perspective to be able to tell the difference between magnetic north and True North—and that made all the difference.

My prayer is that this book will help you sink your roots deeper and make your wings stronger. I pray that each of you has a "hang in there" attitude—that you will be able to hang in, hang on, hang out, hang loose, but never hang it up. Don't ever quit on your dreams. They are the reason you are here and the reason you have this book in your hands.

Learn from what we learned and experienced. Understand why World Wide values what it does. Apply this wisdom to your life. Dig your roots deeply into these things, because that will make your wings stronger. Roots give you the foundation to reach your branches into the sky and bear good fruit.

I am grateful for each person reading this book. I hope you find it helpful, and I can't wait to see how high you will fly.

One of the greatest things
we can do for another person is
teach them to dream, because most people
have lost their dream. Most people
have been beaten down and are hurting.
Somehow, through the process
and the grind of life, they just kind
of gave it up. One of the greatest gifts
we can give another person is to allow
them—just one more time—to hope. . . .

When you put a dream out
in front of a person, you give them
great encouragement.

—JOHN C. MAXWELL

PRINCIPLE #1

YOUR PAST DOESN'T DETERMINE

YOUR FUTURE.

YOUR ABILITY TO DREAM

AND YOUR WILLINGNESS

TO GROW AND WORK WILL

LAY THE FOUNDATION

FOR THE BUSINESS AND LIFE

YOU WANT.

1

It's About Where You're Going More Than Where You've Been

If you'd seen us back when, I doubt you'd think that Ron and I would ever amount to much. Certainly, few people we grew up around did.

I was raised in a tiny farming and lumber community in central Idaho. Grangeville had a population of about 3,600. I had what most people would consider a fairly normal childhood. My earliest memories are of dolls and blanket forts in the backyard with the neighbor kids. I devotedly shadowed my one wonderful sister, Kathy, who always seemed to have cool friends and clothes, and our house was always filled with the aroma of Mom's cooking and baking. Just a whiff of fresh bread still takes me back to those times.

Growing up, I knew that my mom and dad loved me, but I can't recall being told that or receiving many physical displays of affection. My parents were from a sterner background.

Mom loved us by being there for Kathy and me, no matter what was going on in our lives. From as early as I can remember until the day I left for doctor's assistant school in Seattle, Mom was always my anchor to what was good in the world. Dad was a provider who ran his life (and ours) with an attention to detail that was a credit to his German heritage. He was always the strictest of disciplinarians, and he had a tongue he inherited from our rough-and-tumble grandfather. His style was probably honed to perfection by one of his boot-camp drill sergeants. He loved the outdoors and taught us to appreciate the simple beauty of being in nature.

A lot of people think you've made it when you own a business, but that wasn't the case for my parents. Although they owned the only sporting goods store in a town where everyone loved to hunt and fish, both Dad and Mom worked long hours to make it profitable. In many ways, the store ran them, not the other way around. Whatever sense of the American dream my parents had, I don't think it included a bigger home, travel, or owning nice things. Under my parents' roof we always had enough, but not much more.

Ron grew up in the Pacific Northwest. His family lived in Oregon until he was middle school age, when his parents opened a dry cleaner in Cottonwood, about a fifteen-minute drive from Grangeville. When he was a high school junior, they had to shutter their business and move to Grangeville. I first noticed Ron when he was a senior and a varsity basketball player and I was in eighth grade. In small towns like Grangeville, everyone supports high school sports, and star athletes are local heroes. Because Ron was a good player, everyone in town seemed to know him.

Ron was born not long before his dad joined the Navy to fight in World War II. While his dad was in the Navy, his mom started a laundry service to help make ends meet. She'd leave Ron in his crib while she worked. She used to tell the story of how she'd hear the wheels of his crib squeaking on the floor as she worked, and she'd look up to see he'd scooted it into the doorway to observe what she was doing. It's fair to say he was a mover and shaker from the beginning, though it would take a while to rediscover that trait after we were married.

With no local prospects for work after high school, Ron enlisted in the Army. He never tasted beef until he entered basic training. Any meat he'd eaten before that was either hooked or hunted. After boot camp, he was stationed in Germany. He had enlisted in the short window between the Korean and Vietnam wars, so he never had to fight. I think it's one of the reasons he was always so grateful to the veterans who had seen conflict and so thankful for the freedom we have as a result. He never took it for granted.

> "Who's that little cheerleader down there in the middle?"
> "That's one of the Pfeffer girls."
> "Mom, I'm going to marry her."

A couple years after I noticed Ron, he became aware of me. It was an *It's a Wonderful Life* moment. During the winter of my junior year, he returned to Grangeville on leave. During this break, Ron and his mother attended a high school basketball game. Sitting up in the bleachers, Ron leaned over to his mom and asked, "Who's that little cheerleader down there in the middle?"

"That's one of the Pfeffer girls."

"Mom, I'm going to marry her."

That cheerleader was, of course, me.

After the game, Ron introduced himself and asked me out. I was flattered, but I was going steady with another guy at the time, so I turned him down.

But Ron was never one to give up easily.

He went back to Germany but came home on leave the following summer. When he returned, he came looking for me. This time I wasn't dating anyone, so I agreed to go out with him. I was flattered he had remembered me, and I was slightly awestruck by this tall, handsome man in uniform.

Our first date was out to the movies. Ron stood out from the boys I'd dated before. He was so polite, considerate, and generous. I knew soldiers made next to nothing, but he always seemed to have enough to splurge on me. We dated a few more times before he reported to Fort Lewis, just outside of Tacoma, Washington. When he finished with his service that September, he returned to Grangeville and asked me out again. From then on, we were almost inseparable.

> *My parents appreciated that Ron was polite and kept himself well-groomed, but in those early years, they had an issue with his family being from "the wrong side of the tracks."*

My parents appreciated that Ron was polite and kept himself well-groomed, but in those early years, they had an issue with his family being from "the wrong side of the tracks." They looked down on him because he worked at the sawmill instead of behind a desk. They simply didn't think he was good enough for their daughter. Ron's dad's debts at the sporting goods store didn't help either. Ron's dad had a tendency to buy on credit and then constantly ask for extensions on repaying the debt. My dad didn't think much of him as a result. Ron was very good to me, though, so my parents let him hang around, probably hoping I'd tire of him, as I had my other beaus.

I didn't.

Ron was kind, polite, and quiet, which was fine with me. He was never pushy. Even though he didn't have much money, he always gave me wonderful gifts. One Christmas, he gave me an engraved Black Hills gold pin. I still have it, and most of the other little gifts he gave me over the years.

When I graduated from high school in June of 1962, Ron tried to give me an engagement ring, but I turned him down. I loved Ron and wanted to marry him, but I was worried about what my parents— especially Dad—would say. He'd always been very negative about Ron, and I still feared his champion tongue-lashings. I really don't know what I was thinking. Looking back, I'm embarrassed by it today. I should have been braver about it, but I was only eighteen. I had a lot of growing up to do.

That fall, I went to school in Seattle to become a doctor's assistant. I loved it. I lived downtown in the YWCA and walked back and forth to school. Each day after classes, I worked as an elevator operator in a big office building. Back then, the streets in Seattle were as safe as Grangeville's, so I never had any problem walking anywhere, at any hour. It's amazing to think how much times have changed.

Every Saturday night, I called Ron collect from a pay phone. After a few months, I had to stop calling his home because his parents were so annoyed at him for spending nearly his whole paycheck on long distance calls. When I came home for Christmas, we started dating again.

One evening, as we chatted in his car, Ron pulled out the engagement ring and asked me to marry him again. This time I said yes. He seemed so happy putting the ring on my finger. But I was still a coward. I slid the ring off and put it in my pocket after he took me home, so my parents wouldn't see it. Once in my bedroom, I hid the ring in a drawer. My parents never suspected. When Ron would pick me up for a date, I'd sneak it out of the drawer and back onto my finger as I walked out of the house.

I knew I couldn't go through the "ring routine" forever, so the night before I returned to school, I told my parents that Ron and I were engaged. I don't remember how they reacted. Maybe they were a little dumbfounded, but I was on a bus back to Seattle the next day, back to my studies.

I was enrolled in a two-year program, but I missed Ron and my home so much that I finished in ten months. I was a C student in high school, but I got straight A's in Seattle. I'd finally found something I was motivated to learn. It's really amazing what you can accomplish when you set your mind to it.

I moved back to Grangeville in June of 1963. I found a job at a nearby hospital, and Ron and I started planning our wedding.

About a month before the wedding, I was sitting on the "green banana" chair in Mom and Dad's house. The announcements were sent, the wedding gown was purchased, the bridesmaids' dresses were made, and everything was set for the big day. Except for my parents' attitude. Out of the blue, Mom looked straight at me and said, "I'll bet you one hundred dollars that you and Ron never accomplish or do anything successful in your married life."

It was so mean and out of character that I didn't know how to respond. My dad said things like this, but not my mom.

Years later, I wondered if Mom remembered making that bet. I realized she was expressing a mother's concern, but her words got my blood boiling. I was so hurt. I never mentioned it to Ron until we'd been married about ten years, but I can tell you that it lit a fire under me to prove her wrong. Somehow, someway, I was determined to show my parents they were wrong about Ron. We were going to accomplish more than they had ever hoped to.

> *Mom looked straight at me and said, "I'll bet you one hundred dollars that you and Ron never accomplish or do anything successful in your married life."*

I was determined to make sure Mom's comment wouldn't put a damper on our wedding. It didn't. It was wonderful. We got married on Sunday, November 3, 1963, at the Grangeville Methodist Church.

Before the wedding, Ron placed a down payment on a trailer home that was parked in the middle of a weedy field. The rent was next to nothing. The trailer was ten feet wide and fifty-five feet long. It was basically one long hallway, but it was *ours*. And it was the start of a marriage that lasted for more than fifty years.

After our honeymoon, Ron went back to work at the sawmill, and I got a job transcribing patient charts at a doctor's office in Cottonwood. We had only one car, Ron's Corvair Monza, so I drove it every day, while Ron rode to work with friends.

We didn't have much, but we were finally together. It didn't matter what anyone else thought about us. We dreamed of making a go at life, and we were determined to do it well.

The trouble was, we just didn't know how . . . yet.

IT ALL STARTS WITH A DREAM

When mother eagles need to coax their eaglets from the nest so they can learn to fly, they sometimes bring food to an adjacent tree (or adjacent cliff), rather than directly to the nest. This tactic encourages the young eagles to leave the nest and try their wings. (Most eaglets are eager to fly, but some of them need a bit of positive reinforcement to get them out of their comfort zone before they'll give it a try.)

Don't many of us have our own comfort zones that can be just as difficult to leave? It might be living in our parents' home or working for someone else. In a comfort zone, it's easy to dream about what the future might hold, but those dreams will never happen while we're still in the nest. Something has to coax us out. I've seen how the Lord often provides unexpected motivators in our lives—like my mother's $100 bet that Ron and I would never succeed. These motivators often "build a little fire under us," which forces us from our comfort zones. Without an unexpected motivator, Ron and I would never have been able to seek the dreams God placed in our hearts. No risk, no reward. I've never heard a success story from someone who never got out of their comfort zone.

> *I once heard someone say, "You never change until the pain of staying the same is greater than the pain of changing."*

Of course, sometimes the motivation comes from negative reinforcement. I once heard someone say, "You never change until the pain of staying the same is greater than the pain of changing." But change is where we grow.

In the years after we married, Ron and I experienced things that challenged our dreams and forced us to consider whether we were willing to grow to meet the challenge. Many give up when they face hardships. Obstacles always present a choice: Do you want to stay the person you are and compromise your dreams? Or are you willing to grow into the person you need to become to accomplish those dreams?

Ron was never willing to give up on his dreams for our family, even when I fought him on them. He was always willing to learn and grow. It was probably the characteristic that won him the most respect from those who knew him well. No matter how much he succeeded, he was always hungry to learn and grow toward the next dream. And he always encouraged everyone around him to do the same.

Growth is never easy, but there is no better way to live. I believe this will be as true for you as it was for Ron and me. Comfort zones are great places to relax occasionally, but no place to build your life.

When Ron and I started out, we had a dream of the life we wanted, but not a vision of how we'd get there. We didn't want much. A nice house, a decent car, good work with good people helping others, and a family of our own. We were ready to sign on the dotted line for the American dream, to help make the world a better place. We wanted something we could build together. Something that would provide for us, something we could pass on to our kids and their families. And we hoped we could earn a little extra to help us enjoy the journey. Though we had nothing when we got married, we had dreams for something better in the future. That carried us a long way.

No one has ever accomplished anything great or pushed through hardship without a dream for something better on the other side. No one achieves dreams by accident. Dreams keep us from being complacent and sleepwalking through life. To accomplish a dream, you must leave your comfort zone, take some risks, and strive for something more.

You must do the things non-dreamers are unwilling to do. You have to separate yourself from the pack.

Ron and I believe that God created us with a seed of Himself within us. He wanted us to be co-creators with Him. If we're not growing toward some goal or aspiration, we stagnate. If we don't live for something greater than ourselves, we never build lives of adventure and achievement. People who stop dreaming usually trade their ambitions for empty pleasures that slowly eat away at their hopes and dreams. They drink too much, distract themselves with entertainment, abuse drugs, give in to pornography, or fall into other self-destructive behaviors.

Ron illustrated this point with two circles, a smaller circle inside of a larger one. The larger circle is filled with our dreams and aspirations. These are the things we hope to have in our lives, the things we want to accomplish, and the legacy we hope to leave to the world, especially our children and grandchildren. We all want to create something that others will respect—to be an example of a better way to live. It's something that Ron and I believe has been knit into our DNA by God Himself.

As we encounter challenges and obstacles, we face a choice: Do we grow the smaller circle to overlap the bigger circle of our dreams, or do we shrink the circle of our dreams to fit into the smaller circle of who we are at the moment? This decision carries a lot of trade-offs. We choose to grow every day, or we lapse into a life of compromising our dreams.

Dreamers need to grow constantly and remain teachable in order to reach the next level. Non-dreamers? We don't need to address that. I don't think non-dreamers will ever read this book.

To be a Dreamer, you must have desire. Ron and I believe you won't fulfill your God-given potential without it. Desire is the starting point. It gives you the ability to dream in the first place.

Another trait that separates Dreamers from non-dreamers is optimism. Dreamers have a positive attitude. Non-dreamers tend to be negative and let obstacles obscure possibilities. They see all of the "cannots" and "won't works." Non-dreamers want to stay on the safe and well-trodden path of mediocrity.

A dream cannot survive in an infertile, negative mind, so how do you turn an infertile mind into a fertile one? You feed it with possibilities. You keep learning. You hang out with other Dreamers. You keep feeding and growing your dream so no one can steal it. You find pictures that represent your dream and put them where you'll see them every day. You keep your dream at the forefront of your mind. (This is part of engaging daily in behaviors that we in World Wide Dreambuilders call "Being CORE.")

These things will preserve your dreams and give them the chance to survive until you grow into the person who can accomplish them. You need to up your game to meet the challenges and overcome the obstacles of getting where you want to go. You must become the person of your dreams, armed with the necessary knowledge, skills, and courage to inhabit your dreams. You must acquire the personal attributes you need for success.

Always keep your "why" alive. That's the inspiration for your dreams. If you nurture the "why," the "how" will follow.

If you want to succeed, you must fan the flames of your dreams. You breathe life into your dreams by constantly learning and growing and hanging out with other Dreamers. Then it's just a matter of time before you have what you've been hoping for and can move on to dreaming even bigger!

PRINCIPLE #2

EVERY ADVERSITY HOLDS A SEED

OF A GREATER BENEFIT.

WHEN ADVERSITY CLOSES ONE DOOR

OF OPPORTUNITY,

ARE YOU WILLING TO PUSH OPEN

A BETTER ONE?

2

Don't Let Anything Steal
Your Dream

Ron used to say that if you have a dream for your life, you can be happy.

As a young couple starting out, we had nothing but a dream of what our lives might be someday. We were building something together, though at the time we didn't know what. That's usually the point at which, if you're not careful, the dream-stealers will come in and derail your dreams, steal your happiness, and eat away at your marriage.

When you launch out on your own, adversity will enter your life. For most of us, our parents worked hard to protect us from adversity when we were growing up, so it often surprises us when we become adults. You must have a plan for how to meet it. If you don't, adversity, rather than your dreams, will dictate the terms of your life. That's no way to live.

For Ron and me, the first real adversity we faced was an accident at the sawmill, which almost left him paralyzed for life.

When he'd started at the mill, just a kid fresh out of the military without much work experience, he was given the toughest and lowest-paying job: pulling green chain. "Green" lumber was the fresh stuff, uncured, usually wet, laden with sap, and heavy. Pulling that wood from the trucks onto a conveyor system—"chain"—didn't take much expertise, so it was usually the first job anyone got. It was work no one else wanted to do, something to test the mettle of new hires. If they were up to the task, they would stick. If not, they'd be gone within the week.

Hard work never bothered Ron, but he did want better pay. He quickly figured out that the gyppo loaders (also called gyppo loggers) were the mill's best-paid laborers. They were the ones who loaded the cut lumber into neat stacks on the boxcars so it could be shipped. "Gyppos" weren't paid by the hour like others, but by the boxcar. The faster they loaded, the more they earned.

So when he got a break or it was lunchtime, rather than sitting around and discussing TV shows with coworkers, Ron would observe the gyppos. Then, when he'd gotten the gist of it, he'd spell them for breaks or for lunch. When a gyppo eventually moved on and needed to be replaced, someone told the foreman, "Ron knows how to do it." That was the day he started as a gyppo, just a few months before we were married.

Gyppo loading was hard work. It was also dangerous, because you were constantly stacking heavy lumber as fast as you could. You were constantly hovering at the edge of the dock, about twelve feet above the tracks. One misstep and you would take a nasty fall.

That's what happened to Ron.

Moving too fast one day, he planted his foot on the edge of the dock and lost his balance. He fell and landed on his back on the rails. It's a wonder he lived, let alone got up to walk away.

After a quick trip to the doctor, Ron learned he needed to find a new line of work. As it was, his back bothered him for the rest of his life. Unless you knew him well, though, you'd never have known his back often seized up on him. He never complained about it, he never complained of being sick, and he never let anyone know when he was hurting.

Today, a person with an injury like that might go on permanent work disability and sue the company for not providing a safe working environment. That didn't even enter into Ron's mind. That was just the way he was.

Adversity had planted a decision in our path. Thinking about it, Ron said, "You know who makes the most money at the sawmill? It's not the guys on the loading docks. It's the office manager and the accountant." That was when Ron decided to become a CPA. It might sound strange, but we later thanked God for that accident. Had that not happened, who knows how long he would have stayed at the sawmill. We may never have left Grangeville. We wouldn't have built the business or founded World Wide Dreambuilders.

> *Adversity had planted a decision in our path. . . . Had that not happened, who knows how long Ron would have stayed at the sawmill. We may never have left Grangeville.*

Ron began taking accounting correspondence courses. When he learned there was a good business school in Spokane, Washington, we packed our meager possessions in our single-wide "hallway" and hit the road.

That fall, he started at Kinman Business University. I found a job working for a finance company called Fairway Finance, and Ron worked mornings, nights, and weekends all the way through his schooling. I also began selling Avon. Ron would drive me around in the cruddy neighborhood that was my territory and then sit in the car and study while I made my rounds. It was a way to make a tiny bit more money while he finished school.

Ron finished the eighteen months of coursework in just less than a year. He got all A's, except for one B-plus. Once he had his degree, he put on a suit and tie and went to work as an internal auditor at a savings and loan in Spokane, a firm that included approximately twenty regional branches. Part of his job was to travel one week a month to audit these branches. When my parents heard this, they finally deemed him worthy of being part of our family. Their son-in-law was now a successful banker, not some backwoods sawmill worker. It was as if we had "arrived."

> *We would drive around to look at homes that were for sale. . . . Then we'd dream together: Would we ever be able to afford a home like one of those?*

However, Ron was making only slightly more money than he had at the mill.

The closest thing we had to vacations in those days was to take the car out on the weekends, if we had enough gas. We would drive around to look at homes that were for sale. Not big, palatial homes, but nice, clean homes in good neighborhoods. Then we'd dream together: Would we ever be able to afford a home like one of those?

We rarely went out to movies. Our big treat, once a month, was to find a place where we could get fifty-cent hamburgers. That was our big splurge. Beyond that, there was never money for anything more than keeping up with our bills. We took pride, at least, in not falling behind on our monthly payments.

As Ron traveled from branch to branch, he learned how the bank ran. The top spot he could aspire to was branch manager. At one of the branches, Ron found a role model in one of the managers. This guy was as sharp as a tack. He was friendly and jovial—just a neat guy. He'd been with the firm for ten years and belonged to the local country club. Ron always loved golf, so to him this man exemplified the pinnacle of success. Every time Ron visited, he'd make sure he could spend time talking with this manager about how he did things. Just like he had at the sawmill, rather than sitting back and hoping for a lucky break, Ron learned about the position he wanted to advance into. This principle always helped Ron grow, regardless of the job he was doing.

Ron's dream of following in this man's footsteps stalled, however, as he learned more details. While auditing the manager's branch, Ron found some discrepancies in the petty cash. When he confronted him about it, the manager confessed that when they were short at home, he'd borrow money from the petty cash to pay his bills. Then he would replace the funds when he got his next paycheck. Ron was dumbfounded. *Short at home? He belongs to the country club! How could he be short on paying his bills?*

"Why are you a member of the country club if you're short on money?" Ron asked.

"Oh, the savings and loan pays for the country club membership," the manager confided. "That way I can hang out with the wealthier folks in town and, hopefully, get them to bank with us." Despite his charm and optimism, this branch manager was as broke and struggling as we were, just at a slightly higher level.

Digging a little deeper, Ron found out why. Branch managers made only $900 a month. Ron was floored. He was making $475 a month, so it was going to take him ten years to work up to $900! That wasn't much of a future.

It was a wake-up call. Ron was a twenty-five-year-old auditor, calling an older, established branch manager on the carpet. It took him a heartbeat to figure out he didn't want to be like that guy anymore. It was a crushing blow. Feeling bad for him, Ron told the manager he wouldn't turn him in if he never did it again. The manager agreed.

As soon as Ron got home, he put his name in with an employment agency. Soon, the agency got Ron an interview with a government contractor in the Tri-Cities. They were managing support services for the Hanford Project, a nuclear production complex.

The interview went well. A manager told him, "Ron, we'd like to hire you, but we have one problem."

Ron asked, "What's that?"

"Well, down here," he pointed to the application, "you put 'expected wages' to start at $650 a month."

Ron blanched. He thought he'd asked for too much.

Before he was able to say he'd take less, the manager said, "I have to start you at no less than $800, 'cause I'm hiring all these college graduates for $800 a month. With your experience, I've got to at least put you where I'm starting them."

Ron nodded. "Okay, I can work with that." And so Ron went to work for ITT Federal Support Services.

Our dream was back on track—or so we thought.

Even though we'd just sold the trailer and made a down payment on a house in Spokane, Ron knew our future was elsewhere. So we sold that house and moved to Kennewick. Then we met Jim and Sharon Elliot at a Welcome Wagon event for the neighborhood. We hit it off with Jim and Sharon right away, but they moved to Seattle shortly after that. We stayed in touch, even though we weren't sure if we would ever see them again.

Things started to look up again. After living in a couple of crummy rentals, we made a down payment on a brick house on Morain Street. It was a bit more than we could afford, but we felt we could grow into it.

The Hanford nuclear facility operated on a cost-plus-fixed-fee contract with the government. That meant the contractor hired the labor, and the more they hired, the more money the government paid them. It was the crazy kind of deal only a government would put up with. Inflating wages was just the first area of waste and mismanagement Ron saw. The project had 20,000 employees when he started. Two years later, when they were down from three reactors to one, they still had 20,000 employees. Ron asked his boss, "How can we have the same number of people with one-third of the work to do?" His boss told him, "Don't worry about it. You'll have a job here the rest of your life."

Government work is security, right? Ron made the mistake of believing him.

> *His boss told him, "Don't worry about it. You'll have a job here the rest of your life.". . . Of course, the next year, the company lost their contract. Ron and 1,500 other workers were given pink slips.*

Of course, the next year, the company lost their contract. Ron and 1,500 other workers were given pink slips on a Monday, informing them that Friday would be their final workday. "Hey," management said, "it's been great having you work for us! Sorry we can't do anything for you. Good luck."

In the end, our increased income had gotten us into more debt and a bigger mortgage payment. Ron needed a new job right away, and the local job market had just been flooded with 1,500 people looking for work.

Ron went job-hunting immediately. One opportunity was in New Jersey. Ron flew out for an interview, but he decided he didn't want to raise our kids in the heart of a city.

> *We were in over our heads, so my dream of being a stay-at-home mom now seemed impossible. . . . Here was adversity knocking at our door again.*

Fortunately, there was a public utility district that needed a treasurer and office manager right away. Ron applied and got the job, but with the glut of people looking for work, wages had been driven down. Ron would make 30 percent less. We were in over our heads, so my dream of being a stay-at-home mom now seemed impossible. (Jim was born before we left Spokane. Brian came along soon after we moved to the Tri-Cities.) My world was Ron, our two little guys, and our home. I loved it, but here was adversity knocking at our door again, threatening all of that.

I needed to find a job to make ends meet. We didn't want some stranger raising our kids, so we came up with a plan. I'd watch the kids during the day and work nights. Ron could come home from work and watch the boys during the evenings. My best option was waitressing, although I didn't have any experience.

There was a Denny's near our house. I went in and, following Ron's advice, offered to work a trial week for just tips. The manager agreed. He gave me a slot on the graveyard shift. At the end of the week, I got the job. I eventually worked up to swing shift so I didn't have to be away all night.

Each morning, we rose together, and then Ron rushed off to work. When he returned home at night, I took the car to Denny's. I'd work until midnight or 1:00 AM on weekdays and the day shift on Saturdays. Ron called it our sixteen-hour-a-day divorce.

To help out even more, I started caring for a family's three boys while their mom went to work. She worked early, so she dropped off her kids before sunrise. I'd get the two oldest ones ready and off to school, then take care of her youngest. Every morning when she left, all I could think was how much I never wanted to do that with our children. The thought made me want to cry.

Our dreams of family, financial well-being, and Ron finding a satisfying career—let alone having anything extra for enjoying life—were slowly crumbling. But what could we do? We had to figure out how to make it work. It would be temporary, right? Ron would eventually find something better or get a raise, and we'd be back on our feet.

Instead, we faced more adversity.

We were living a double life. Ron was experiencing the full weight of working for a company that considered him a cog in their machine, not a person. He was already the treasurer, comptroller, and office manager, but when upper management decided to automate their systems with computers, they said, "Well, Ron can do that."

Ron didn't know anything about computers or even what "automation" meant, but it was now part of his job. More pressure, more of a workload, more responsibility—and all for the same pay, of course.

Ron took a two-week crash course in computer billing and began working to automate all systems and business records, without shirking his other responsibilities. There just weren't enough hours in the workday. So what did he do? He doubled down and started going in earlier in the mornings to work three or four hours before his normal shift started. He worked whenever I wasn't working. Our already-meager family time was now gone.

Then Ron's dad passed away. Ron was the oldest son, so he believed caring for his mother was his responsibility. And he was the only one in his family who was in a position to help. So, in addition to the debt we were already accumulating, we had to take out a second mortgage to pay off his parents' loans.

Taking on that debt meant every cent of our salaries was accounted for before the month began. Our only "disposable income" were my Denny's tips, and that became our food budget. Ron began waiting up for me, no matter how late I worked, so we could count my tips at our rickety kitchen table before we went to bed. He used to joke that he would grab me by the ankles and turn me upside down to shake me each night, just to make sure we hadn't missed any coins. Since that was our grocery money, if I had a bad night serving eggs and bacon to the guys who came in tipsy (or worse) after hanging out at the bars, it meant less food in the fridge for the week.

Ron had just turned thirty, and he later told me that when we'd go to bed, he couldn't sleep. Instead, he'd lie wide awake and look at the ceiling, wondering if his life was over. The pressure was eating away at our marriage. We couldn't talk about money without fighting, and we hardly ever saw each other except for trading keys in the driveway when he came home from work and I headed for Denny's.

Sometimes, Ron would break out in a cold sweat and ask himself, *Is this all there is to life? Everything's a mess. My wife's working nights, we never have any family time, we're in debt up to our ears, my career is heading nowhere, and all Georgia Lee and I do is pick at each other.*

What do I have left to live for? he wondered.

Without realizing how we'd gotten there, we were living what Henry David Thoreau called "the life of quiet desperation." At best, our dreams were on life support, and we were in denial about it. We were in a prison of debt. Everything we were earning was already promised to someone else, for years into the future. All we could do was tie one more knot at the end of our rope and hope it would be the one we could hang on to. Surely things couldn't go on like this forever, could they?

> *Disappointment is a form of adversity—as are all of the dream thieves. What will you do with your disappointment?*

Something had to give.

Thank God something did. Jim and Sharon Elliot reconnected with us.

AVOIDING THE DREAM THIEVES

Five things can steal your dream if you let them.

The first is disappointment. Of course, you can't avoid disappointment. If you work with people, you're going to be disappointed. There's an old saying among pastors: "Ministry would be great if it weren't for the people."

Well, ministry is people, and so is business. If you work with people, you will be disappointed, because people have different priorities. They are going to do things you don't expect them to do. That's just the way things are, and that's why it's easy to become disappointed.

However, when you experience disappointment, take it as a comma, not a period. There's something on the other side. Pause, think, and reevaluate where you are, rather than getting stuck in your tracks. Disappointment is a form of adversity—as are all of the dream thieves. What will you do with your disappointment? (Hint: If you want to realize your dreams, remove "quitting" from your list of options.)

Dad would always say . . .

Here's something Dad told me when I would whine about not being where I wanted to be because my downline was not doing what I thought they should be doing: "Jim, it is not your downline's fault that you aren't where you want to be. It is your fault. They don't work for you. If you are not where you want to be, *you* have not done enough work and sponsored enough people. Stop whining and get to work. You want more? Then go help more people."

—Jim

Disappointment isn't the only obstacle you will face. Right behind it is rejection. We all experience rejection in life. The bigger your dream, the more likely you are to experience rejection. Not everyone wants to do more. That is their choice. If they don't want to join you, find those who do. The more you want to accomplish, the more people you may need to go through to find those who want to join you. The only way that will be a negative for you is if you insist that everyone be exactly like you. Don't reject another person's right to be different.

Now, some people are not satisfied with just saying, "No, thank you." They will try to tear you down. Some people seem to think that by diminishing others they elevate themselves. What they don't realize (and what you must realize) is that they are not rejecting you. They are exposing themselves. The only way they can harm you is if you agree with them.

Take it in stride. Tell yourself, "I am grateful that they showed me who they are up-front so I didn't waste a lot of time getting invested in them." Keep doing what you know is right. This will help you grow toward your dream.

When you decide to be a Dreamer, people of low character are going to mock you. When you'd rather sit in the corner of the lunchroom and read a motivational book than sit and talk about what some Hollywood celebrity just did, coworkers are going to give you a hard time. They've given up on their dreams, and it makes them uncomfortable to see someone else chasing theirs.

Dreamers and non-dreamers don't speak the same language. But you're not responsible to them. There's a reason you have the dreams you do. Beyond that, your spouse and your family are the ones counting on you. Why would you worry about what anyone else thinks beyond that?

Treasure your dream. Hang on to it. Fight for it.

A third thing to watch out for is failure. You're going to see people further along the way, those closer to achieving their dreams than you are. It's going to feel like you're moving so slowly that you'll never get there. You might see someone who's accomplished great things in the business you're just starting out in, and you have no idea how to get to where they are now. It seems so far away. On top of that, you might do something foolish and mess up. You're not making baby steps toward your dream anymore; you're moving *backward*.

You're going to feel like you'll never get where you want to go. It will make you want to quit. Take heart. We've all been there. We've done dumb things more than once. (*Way more than once.*)

Let me encourage you: For every success Ron and I experienced while building our business, we've had at least three failures. But, like us, you will always have a choice: You can accept your failure as final and quit, or you can learn from it and do things smarter next time. You can tell yourself that your failure means *you* are a failure, or you can tell yourself, *Well, there's a lesson learned, and I'm better for it. I'll never do that again, or at least not in the same way. With each mistake I experience, I learn something new. As long as I keep learning, I'm moving forward.*

As a rule, success is built on failure. Thomas Edison tried thousands of different filaments before finding the one that made his light bulb work. That's a thousands-to-one failure-to-success ratio, but that one success meant "Let there be light" for the entire world. Edison said, "Many of life's failures are people who did not realize how close they were to success when they gave up."

Abraham Lincoln suffered both professional and personal tragedies in his life. He was involved in a failed business. When he was elected president of the United States, seven states seceded from the union. Four more followed on the day of his inaugural address. Two of his sons died very young. Yet today he is still considered among the greatest—if not the greatest—president in American history. It's not your failures that matter, but what you do after them.

Don't let failures be stumbling blocks. Make them stepping-stones instead. When asked how many times he failed, Thomas Edison answered, "I have not failed. I've just found thousands of ways that won't work." Failure builds character. Ron and I believe that God will often use failure to prune things out of our lives that would destroy us if they were still around when success finally came. Overcoming failure refines us and our attitudes. It creates endurance. It produces character. It teaches us how to laugh at ourselves. And when you can laugh at your failures, you're taking good steps toward success.

The fourth thing that can steal your dream is opposition. People will stand against you, and if you're in this business, you don't have to search far to find horrible things written about Amway and those

> *If you're part of the masses, if you're just a wandering generality taking the path of least resistance, non-dreamers are going to be just fine with you. But if you want to be a* meaningful specific? *You must have a dream you're willing to fight for.*

who've succeeded at it. (It's written from misunderstandings, at best. Most of the statements are written by people who've never been in the business or never really committed to it. That's just the nature of things. It's a lot easier to criticize something to get attention than it is to succeed at it and get recognition for that.)

Any time someone tries to stand for something, do something, or gain something worth having, he or she will face opposition. On the other hand, if you don't want to know something, do something, or have anything, nobody will oppose you. They'll leave you alone. If you're part of the masses, if you're just a wandering generality taking the path of least resistance, non-dreamers are going to be just fine with you.

But if you want to be a *meaningful specific*? You must have a dream you're willing to fight for. Do you want to leave your fingerprints on the world in a positive way? Then be willing to withstand opposition. Victor Hugo once wrote, "You have enemies? Why, it is the story of every man who has done a greet deed or created a new idea. It is the cloud which thunders around everything that shines. Fame must have enemies, as light must have gnats. Don't bother yourself about it. . . ."

The fifth and final thing to be wary of is success itself. Yes, you read that right. In the same way that "nothing succeeds like success," nothing can derail long-term success like thinking you know what you are doing because of short-term victories. Ron's favorite definition of success was: "Success is the progressive realization of a worthwhile goal." It is a journey, not a destination. You stop being a success when you stop being successful. You don't arrive at success. You arrive at failure.

Too many reach a goal and say to themselves, "Man, look at me! Aren't I great? Look what I did!" What they did is nice, but they're only starting out. The things required at one level are rarely the same abilities, skills, and knowledge you will need to succeed at the next level. Never let pride sneak in and tell you that you can stop growing. It doesn't work like that. If you want to keep succeeding on greater levels, then the only time to stop growing is when you move on to Heaven.

Dad would always say . . .

"It is one thing to go Diamond and
another to stay Diamond."

—Jim

Never lose your humility. The root of the word humility is *humus* or "rich, healthy soil." To be *humble,* then, is to remain "grounded," with your dreams planted in a fertile mind. Ron and I chose to live believing that our achievements are founded upon the God we follow and the principles we hold dear. To be humble is to remember where you came from and who gave you your success. If you think you've arrived and it's time to relax and enjoy life—to "eat, drink, and be merry"—then you are simply dreaming too small or thinking it's all about you. It's not. The impression you leave on the universe is always about what you do for others. It's about living to give to others, not taking all you can get.

Success is a journey that starts the day you're born and continues until the day you die. Never stop dreaming. When you accomplish one dream, get a bigger one. You'll find that, if you keep your eyes on serving other people and loving people, life will be wonderfully new with each dream you accomplish. Each new level you reach in your business will give you time and resources to help others start reaching for their dreams. Let me tell you: Once you start doing that, life will take on qualities you've never imagined.

That's when you'll realize there are things worth fighting for. You won't take your new dreams or the dreams of others lightly. You won't take your freedoms lightly, you won't take your country lightly, you won't take your beliefs lightly (for Ron and I, that meant our faith in God), you won't take your spouse lightly, and you won't take those in this business lightly. They all become more important as you dream bigger and bigger. You realize where you would be if not for taking hold of your dream. (Ron and I also believed we benefited a great deal from God's grace as well!) Then you'll realize it was worth hanging on to your dreams despite the disappointments, rejections, opposition, and failures. You won't let yourself be fooled into pride by short-term successes. You'll keep chasing dreams that are worth holding on to, and you will truly live your life.

PRINCIPLE #3

A DREAM IS A DESTINATION.

A VISION IS YOUR

ROAD MAP FOR GETTING THERE.

YOUR DREAM WILL PERISH

IF IT NEVER BECOMES A VISION.

3

Turning Your Dream into a Vision

I've heard it said that, sometimes, instead of leading us by opening up opportunities, God closes doors to force us to find a better way. I think that's what happened for Ron and me, even though we didn't know the Lord at that point in our lives. Backed into a corner in our careers, and with our financial future looking bleak, God opened an opportunity for us to get back into the life He wanted for us. I thank Him every day that one of us recognized this opportunity for what it was.

During November of 1971, Jim Elliot called Ron and asked if he and his wife could show us a business we might be interested in.

Of course, we wouldn't be interested. What was he thinking? That we were hard up for money or something?

Oh, the things pride tells you. As the saying goes, "Denial is not just a river in Egypt."

"Well, we'd love to see you," Ron told Jim. "You can visit us, but we're not interested in your business. Everything here's going great."

Ron would have flat-out told Jim not to bother, but he was concerned that Jim was into some crazy thing, and his first instinct was to help get him out of it. We hadn't seen this couple in years; what had they gotten themselves into? There was a company selling bras and women's underwear that Ron had been hearing about, and he wondered if that's what Jim was up to. Surely Ron would be able to talk some sense into him.

In the midst of a November storm, Jim and Sharon packed their three kids (all younger than six) into their VW Bug and drove through the mountains and driving snow from Seattle to Kennewick. They arrived Friday night after I had gone to work at Denny's. As you probably remember, I worked swing shift on Friday night, then rose at the crack of dawn to work the day shift on Saturday. It was never my best night.

> "You can visit us, but we're not interested in your business. Everything here's going great."

Once they were settled in at our home, Ron wanted Jim to get through his presentation so they could spend the rest of the evening visiting. However, Jim insisted that both of us hear what he had to say. Even though Ron thought this was silly, he agreed. Ron and the Elliots got the five kids settled for the night and visited while they waited for me to come home.

As usual, I didn't get home until well after midnight. Knowing I would get only a few hours of sleep before going back to work the next morning, I was not in the best of moods when I saw the three of them waiting up for me. Striving to be polite, I sat down by Ron, still somewhat grimy from my shift, and tried to listen graciously.

There was no way I was going to ask any questions. I just wanted it over with. I kept thinking, *Just hurry up and get done so I can go to bed.*

About fifteen minutes into the presentation, Ron asked for the name of the company in question. He told me later he was still worried they were going to ask him to sell bras. He wanted to know before Jim got any further.

"The name is short for 'the American Way,'" Jim told us. "It's the Amway Corporation."

Amway? My eyes must have widened to the size of saucers. *The A word.* My mind immediately went to the one Amway experience of my life.

A few months previously, a man had come to our door, asking if I wanted to buy some laundry soap. He was, to put it kindly, out of shape and grungy. There was a hole in his T-shirt, just to the right of his navel. His hair was unkempt, and he had three days' worth of stubble on his face (which was not in style then like it is today). He carried his product in a little, red wagon—probably his kid's. It was almost frightening. When he asked if I wanted to buy some Amway detergent, I almost slammed the door in his face. Any time I heard the word "Amway" after that, he was the first thing that came to mind.

I didn't want anything to do with the company.

I was out.

"Well, I've got an early shift in the morning," I announced unceremoniously. "I need to get some sleep. Good night, all!"

And I was gone.

I didn't give it another thought.

They were our guests for the evening, and I didn't even get their bed ready. I didn't show them where the towels were or do anything to make them feel welcome or comfortable.

I'm sure Ron was mortified, but what could he do? He could either make a big scene or let it go, and Ron was never one for big scenes.

It was not my best moment.

I didn't care. I wasn't about to peddle soap door-to-door like that beggarly looking man. They were crazy if they thought I was like that. *What could they have been thinking? Don't they think we have any dignity?*

It didn't matter. The minute my face hit the pillow, I was asleep.

Early the next morning, I woke up, got myself ready, donned my waitress outfit, and marched down the hallway, headed for the door.

As I came around the corner into the main living area, Jim and Ron were at the sink, mixing something in a glass with a spoon. There was no sign of Sharon.

What are those two up to?

I hadn't noticed Ron wasn't in bed beside me when I got up. I had tried so hard not to wake him that I didn't even notice he wasn't there!

I soon realized that the two men had been up all night. And while I was asleep, Jim lit a fire in Ron, a fire I would never be able to extinguish.

Since I hadn't been there for the rest of Jim's presentation, it was impossible to figure out what had happened while I slept, but Ron saw something in Amway that night, something I wouldn't understand for almost a year. Ron got a vision for how to recapture our dreams. He saw a second chance at getting the life we had always talked about, and he wasn't going to let it slip through his fingers without giving it a fair shot.

The men hardly noticed me as I came down the hallway, so I went into the kitchen and opened and closed some drawers and cupboards, putting away the dishes and pots and pans from the night before. When they still failed to notice me, I added a little more oomph to make more of a racket. Finally, I gave them a rather dirty look and marched off to work.

When I returned that evening, Ron tried to convince me that we needed to sign up for the business.

I was far from enthusiastic.

"This will work, Georgia Lee," he told me. "Our family needs what's available through this business."

I turned on the negativity, but it didn't faze him.

He kept at it for the next week.

Finally he said, "Look, Georgia Lee, I'm going to do it with you or without you. I know I can make it work for us."

"Fine," I said. "*Without me. I don't want to have anything to do with it. I'm not going door-to-door like some homeless person to sell soap!*"

"But that's not what they're . . ." He stopped midsentence. It was probably the look on my face. He knew that look. He knew it was time to stop. He'd save his arguments for another time. Better to prove it would work than to try to convince a resistant prospect. That quiet, patient resolve was something Ron would be known for in the decades to come.

> **I turned on the negativity, but it didn't faze him.**

"Okay," he said. "I can do it on my own. It's what's best for our family. The first thing I'm going to do is earn enough money so you won't have to work at Denny's anymore."

I thought he was crazy.

With my salary and tips, I was making about $400 a month. *He is going to make $400 a month selling soap, eh? Good luck with that.*

Ron had his first goal. It was also the first step toward getting our vision for our family back on track. He had no intention of doing more than buying at IBO cost and selling some product to friends, neighbors, and relatives. He just needed $400 a month. He figured he'd just need to find some regular customers to make enough to bring me home to be with the kids again.

Of course, there was more to it than that. When you start a business, people don't automatically show up at your door. You have to go out and let them know about your products and your business. The first hurdle he had to face was his shyness.

As a rule, he never answered the phone. If the doorbell rang, he'd go to the bedroom and wait until I told him who it was. If it was someone he didn't know (or if more than two people showed up), he was hesitant to come out. Ron left the welcoming duties to me, so I wasn't sure how he was going to make presentations and establish customers.

> 66
>
> *As a rule, Ron never answered the phone. If the doorbell rang, he'd go to the bedroom and wait until I told him who it was.*
>
> 99

He was not exactly the person you would pick to lead an organization of tens of thousands of people—at least not when he started out.

And he was already working crazy hours at the PUD, so he didn't want to host meetings alone. The only real free time we had together was Saturday night, so he decided he'd start his business by making one presentation a week on that night. He asked me to be there with him to play hostess, to wear something nice (my only real dress at the time was my Denny's uniform), and to keep my negative comments to myself. Considering his goal was to allow me to stay home with the boys, it was the least I could do.

Now we had to figure out who we were going to invite to these presentations.

Thankfully, before we had to worry about this, Jim offered to help. He told Ron, "Let me come over and help you get your business started."

"Okay, what do I need to do?"

"Why don't you invite all your friends and relatives over to your home so I can show them the plan? If they're interested, I'll work with them for you. You don't have to do it. If they want you to sponsor them, we'll get them started together. If they don't, you can ask them to be retail customers."

"Besides," Jim went on, "if I present for you, at least they'll know what you're doing and not think you're in one of these illegal deals."

That made sense to Ron, and it meant he wouldn't have to speak in front of the group.

"I'll be back next week," Jim told him. "Can you invite some folks over?"

Ron nodded while his stomach knotted. Inviting people to the meeting suddenly seemed almost as daunting as planning to present. Almost.

When you're nervous about something, you put it off. Ron thought all week about picking up the phone to invite folks over for Saturday night, but he didn't do anything about it until Friday after work. Scared to death, he called and made a quick couple of invitations. One thing about Ron, though: He wasn't going to lie or try to fool anyone into anything. He was going to be up-front about everything. When someone asked, "Is this one of those Amway-type things?" Ron said, "No, it *is* Amway." When the line went dead, he tried not to think about it as he dialed the next number.

In the end, Ron convinced one couple to attend.

As we sat there with that couple, drinking coffee and waiting for Jim to arrive, I knew Ron was nervous and embarrassed to have Jim come all the way from Seattle for one couple. Thankfully, when Jim showed up, he was very gracious—even excited.

"Well, I'm a little glad there isn't a big group," he began. "I came mainly for you, Ron. Let's show the plan to this couple, and don't you worry about it. We'll talk the rest of the night about where to go from here."

Ron was floored. He'd never had anyone talk to him like that, to be so supportive. In fact, on Jim and Sharon's previous visit, their VW Bug had broken down on the way back home, and they were forced to ride with the tow-truck driver (with their three kids) from Ellensburg to Seattle so Jim could get to work on Monday. Now Jim was back again, saying he would have shown up to support Ron even if no one had shown up. This was a new experience for Ron. No one had ever shown such interest in his success, not even his parents.

Despite Jim's enthusiasm, the evening quickly took a turn for the worse. About halfway through the presentation, the husband of the couple asked Jim, "Is this Amway?" Jim told him, "Yes." The man rose and told his wife they were leaving. "I don't want anything to do with it," he told Ron. "It's illegal. It's like all those other pyramids." Turns out, he'd heard all the bad and misinformed opinions about Amway and associated it with other schemes that actually were illegal. He and his wife were out the door before Jim or Ron could say anything to correct the misunderstanding.

Still, Jim was unfazed. He sat down with Ron and started talking about next steps: "Now Ron, here's what you do. I'll be back in a month. You go and make presentations one-on-one." Then he walked Ron through how to do a one-on-one presentation. He asked Ron to "practice" on him. He told Ron the first thing he needed to do was focus on creating sales volume and try to get it up to $150 a month. When Jim left that evening, Ron felt like he knew everything he needed to know and do until the month was up and Jim would return for another group meeting.

Ron got "no's" from the first nineteen people he talked to about joining the business, but out of those he earned fifteen retail customers. As Ron got closer to his first goal of replacing my salary, he became increasingly excited about his business's potential.

All the while, I was far from encouraging. I was more interested in telling him, "I told you so," than in seeing him succeed. Looking back, I'm ashamed of how I treated him most of that first year of building *our* business. It's shameful how focused we can get on "being right," rather than supporting those we love.

Because people were ordering product from us, we had to fill the orders. This was a different time, before everything went online, shipping directly from warehouse to consumer. Each Sunday night, before

> " *As Ron got closer to his first goal of replacing my salary, he became increasingly excited about his business's potential.* "

going to bed, Ron would complete all of his order forms for the coming week. Then he would pick up the product from a servicing distributor in town.

It was a lot of work, but Ron didn't care. He was so excited to earn extra money that he started counting the days until I could quit waitressing.

Before Jim visited again, he called Ron to discuss whom to invite to the next meeting: "Hey Ron, why don't you invite some casual acquain-tances? You've gone through most of your friends and relatives, right?"

"Yeah. What's a 'casual acquaintance'?"

"People you know but don't normally socialize with. Do you know anyone who wants to make some extra money on the side?"

Ron answered, "I can think of a few folks."

They started to make a list.

> **Again, Ron waited until the Friday before the meeting to invite anyone.**

Again, Ron waited until the Friday before the meeting to invite anyone.

One of Ron's prospects was a local state examiner who came to the PUD every now and then to audit them. It just so happened that he was there the day before Jim was coming back to do another meeting. At almost 5:00 that Friday afternoon, Ron popped his head into the office where the man was working and said, "Hey Ken, I have a friend who's very successful in a business. It's kind of a new concept. He's wanting to expand it over here in the Tri-Cities, and he's working with me. He wants to work with a few other people too. Would you be interested in dropping in tomorrow night and meeting my wife? I'd like to meet yours too—and I can introduce you to my friend. He can tell you about what we're doing."

Ready for questions or protests, Ron was surprised when Ken simply answered, "Sure, as long as it doesn't have anything to do with selling."

"What do you mean?"

"Well, I was in some kind of a multilevel thing before, and I still have a basement full of their products. My wife is still mad at me over that one."

"Oh no, it's nothing like that," Ron answered. He was right too. The way Amway is set up, the worst you can ever do is buy products you use yourself, at business-owner cost. Amway continues to stand behind their products today with a 180-day, 100 percent satisfaction guarantee.* Ron knew Amway was different from any other multilevel company out there at the time.

So Ken said he would come. With the energy from that, Ron went home and made some calls. A cousin who had been out of town the previous month agreed to attend.

The next night, there were seven of us: Ken, his wife, Ron's cousin and his wife, Jim, Ron, and me. I did my best to look nice, serve coffee, and keep my mouth shut about anything related to the business.

As Jim launched into his presentation, Ron and I sat in the back, behind the others. Ron took my hand as things got started and seemed to hold on for dear life. I could feel his fear that someone would get up and walk out. No one did. When Jim suggested we take a break before answering questions, Ken approached Jim and started asking him about the program. I thought Ron was going to hug him. He was so excited. Ken was the first person to show any interest. The more interest he showed, the more trouble Ron had containing his excitement.

Finally, Ken asked, "What do I need to do next? What's the next step?"

"Well," Jim answered, shooting a sly smile to Ron, "next Saturday night, host a meeting like this in your home. Invite friends, relatives, or whomever you want. Then Ron will come over and show the plan for you."

---

* Some exclusions apply. This satisfaction guarantee does not apply to Partner Store purchases or IBO purchases for stock, inventory, or product kits.

I don't think I've ever seen color fade from a face like it did from Ron's in that instant. *Present the plan to a bunch of strangers?* I thought Ron was going to melt into the floor. But he didn't. He stood his ground and did his best to smile.

Before the end of the night, Ken and his wife, Sarah (who was somewhat reluctant—they still had a basement full of another company's products), were the first people Ron sponsored into the business. Despite Ron's hesitancy to present, Ken and Sarah knew Ron believed in the business. As they would say years later, "Ron always believed in what he was doing. Whenever he talked about this business, we knew he believed the business would grow bigger than the Tri-Cities area."

CONCEIVE AND BELIEVE, THEN ACHIEVE

Ron and I were convinced that God wouldn't force us to fulfill our dream. When He gave us our dream, He also gave us the choice of chasing that dream or letting it die. God gave Ron and I our dream to encourage us to grow. A dream is something beyond what you can accomplish now. It's out there, just beyond your present knowledge, talents, and abilities. It's often not something you can accomplish alone, but it's well within your potential. You just have to grow into it.

As author Napoleon Hill famously said, "Whatever the mind can conceive and believe, it can achieve."

Don't switch that around. "Conceiving" is dreaming. The conception is the dream. That comes first. Then you must believe it is possible, that you can make it happen. Your dream should carry a sense of destiny—that it is something divinely intended for you to do. That is called *vision*.

Conviction makes your mind a fertile place to plant your dream and cultivate it. Keep your dream in a fertile mind until you can gather the knowledge, willpower, and skills that will enable you to see yourself fulfilling that dream. It's tough to do that on your own. You'll need outside help. You need to be a reader. You need to be hungry for motivational and leadership-building talks. You need to be around other Dreamers.

And you need to be mentored by people who have been where you want to go, who have a road map for you. That's how you move beyond just dreaming to doing what it takes to make your dream a reality.

> " *Ron and I knew that God had given us our dream; it was our responsibility to turn it into a vision.* "

Once you believe it, you need a vision for how to go out and achieve it. You need a vision that will motivate you and give you a step-by-step plan to achieve what you've conceived. Ron and I knew that God had given us our dream; it was our responsibility to turn it into a vision.

The first step of the process is desiring your dream with all your heart. Many people set goals based on income. That's how we started, but after a while we found that to be a shallow understanding of a vision. If you want only money, you can turn into an Ebenezer Scrooge, or worse. You might follow the old axiom, "Get all you can, can all you get, then sit on the can." Honestly, that's no way to live.

It's not about money; it's about what money can do for you. It's about the freedom money can bring you. It's about freedom from debt, freedom to choose what you do with your time, freedom to be able to afford things like taking a family vacation or starting an orphanage in Africa, or funding a clinic in Haiti. Money is just a tool. It's neither good nor bad.

In God's economic plan for His people (which we call free enterprise), money is just a measurement of how you are working toward your dreams. Happiness is another, but it's harder to measure. So is the quality of your family life and other relationships.

Here's another way to look at it: Money is a way to keep track of the amount of service we render to others through our business. As a hammer is to a carpenter, money is a Dreamer's tool to achieve what they conceive and believe.

In our case, Ron and I believed that if we used money God's way, He would bless us with opportunities to earn more. If you look at some of the godliest people in the Bible, you will see they were very wealthy because they had dreams from God that they wanted to accomplish. They were walking with God to make the dreams real. Whether it was building a great ark to save the world, establishing a kingdom, or spreading God's message throughout Europe and Asia, money was a tool they used to accomplish the things God was directing them to do.

> **For belief to become faith, you've got to feed it with possibilities, motivation, how-to's, success stories, willpower, character, and work—lots of work.**

The next thing you need to do is believe (with your whole heart and soul) that your dream is worthwhile. Merely desiring something is not enough. You must believe it is worth accomplishing and that you are worthy of accomplishing it. For belief to become faith, you've got to feed it with possibilities, motivation, how-to's, success stories, willpower, character, and work—lots of work.

You must crowd out doubts with "can-do's." If you have questions, get answers. Turn your car and your smartphone into a traveling university. Everywhere you go, listen to things that will motivate and instruct you.

Third, vividly imagine your dream. Write your dream and the steps you'll need to take to accomplish it. Spend your money on paper before you earn it, so you have a picture of what you are hoping for. How will you spend the extra money you earn? What does being free from traditional employment to become a full-time entrepreneur look like? Cut pictures representing those things out of magazines and hang them on your refrigerator. Make a vision board. Constantly keep what you are working for in front of your eyes.

Fourth, enthusiastically talk about your dreams with fellow believers and those who support you. Who wants it for you? First of all, you want it, right? We dream so we can be happy. They're what make life fulfilling. Your spouse and your kids want it for you, because it's going to be a tremendous blessing for them. The people upline from you want it for you, because they know that by helping you get what you need, they will get what they need. You need to enthusiastically talk about it with people who will encourage you. Then—and this is what makes the business so beautiful—you need to understand that you will get what you want only by doing the same for the people downline from you.

Dad would always say . . .

"You don't tell them what *you* want.
You find out what *they* want and help them get it."

—Jim

And who should you avoid engaging in conversation? People who are full of "can't." People who have given up on their own dreams and will be happy if you give up on yours. They are easy to figure out. Sadly, they are often the people closest to us. I was one of those people for a while. Ron knew better than to talk about Amway with me until I "came around." Don't be mean to these folks. Don't shun them either. Be a blessing to them and let them see the beauty of your vision in their own time. Let them ask about it. If they truly care about you, eventually they will ask. If they don't, bless them and keep chasing your dream and enhancing your vision.

When you can do these four things, a dream is no longer a dream. It is a vision. You've given your dream legs. It becomes something you can ride toward success.

A dream isn't enough. A dream is like a parked car sitting next to a curb. If you don't turn on the ignition, put it in gear, hit the accelerator, and get into the flow of traffic, you'll go nowhere. You can believe all you want, but without action, your faith is worthless. Ron and I believe that God doesn't reward faith without works, and a dream without action is just a dream. It's a pretty picture of a place you will never go.

Ron and I also believe that even God can't steer a parked car. He isn't going to put it in gear for you, and He's not going to turn the key for you. He's not going to press the accelerator for you. He gave you the ability to do that. He has His part; you have yours. He gave you the ability to turn your dream into an accomplishable vision.

Isn't it time for your dream to hit the road toward reality?

PRINCIPLE #4

DON'T SETTLE FOR POTENTIAL;

FULFILL IT.

GROW INTO THE PERSON WHO CAN

ACCOMPLISH YOUR DREAM;

THEN FIND A BIGGER DREAM

TO KEEP YOU MOVING FORWARD.

4

Growing Goal by Goal

Ron was set to make his first home presentation, to a group of people he'd never met. He was going to Ken and Sarah Kuklinski's house, to stand in front of a bunch of strangers and tell them about Amway.

He was as white as a ghost as he left the house.

We didn't have a whiteboard or anything for Ron to use for the presentation, so he borrowed a big chalkboard and tripod from the meeting room at the PUD. It was so big that it didn't fit in our Rambler station wagon. He had to tie the back door shut to keep the chalkboard from sliding out.

The meeting was supposed to start a little after 8:00, so Ron left our house at 7:30. We had a bottle of whiskey he kept under the sink for guests and special occasions. He pulled it out, took a big gulp, and put it back before he left.

> ❝
> *About halfway around, on the other side of the block, there was a little park. Ron stopped, got out of the car, and vomited into a bush.*
> ❞

The Kuklinskis lived on the block behind us, so Ron arrived early. Seeing no cars, he decided to circle and come back. No need to be too early and stand around awkwardly talking to people, right? Or stand around talking with Ken alone, if no one showed.

At a quarter till, Ron passed by again. Still no cars. He decided to circle the block again.

Five minutes later, he made another pass. This time, there was a car. Now what was he going to do? He decided to circle again, half hoping the people would change their minds and leave before he got back around.

Five till. Another car. Another circle.

At eight sharp, Ron saw yet another car. It was too much. He circled again.

About halfway around, on the other side of the block, there was a little park. Ron stopped, got out of the car, and vomited into a bush. Then he circled back to the Kuklinskis'.

Another car had arrived. He decided to stop procrastinating, thinking, *I should get in there before anyone else shows up.*

Of course, now he couldn't park in front of the house because of all the cars, so he parked across the street. He pulled out the big chalkboard and the tripod.

The Northwest is known for its wet weather and rain forests, but eastern Washington and Oregon are vast, flat deserts. The Tri-Cities are in that area. A thirty-miles-per-hour wind is considered a breeze, and it's always blowing.

As Ron tucked the blackboard under his arm and started walking across the street, he was met by one of those "breezes."

Fighting the gust, he found himself in front of the Kuklinskis' neighbor's house. Getting to the *correct* front door was like trying to back up a sailboat. Unsure of what to do, he pointed the edge of the blackboard directly into the wind and fought his way forward.

Instead of mosquito mesh, the Kuklinskis' screen door was made of clear glass. Not seeing a doorbell, Ron opened the screen gingerly so he could knock. The minute he got a grip on the handle, a wind gust caught the door and ripped it out of his hand. The door smashed against the house, shattering into a million pieces. (I know that sounds crazy, but you can't make this stuff up.)

Sarah's voice rang out inside the house: "What in the he** is going on out there?" She opened the door and gave Ron a look that would have turned hot tea to ice, even on a July day.

Ron gulped. "Can I come in?"

She looked at him, at the remains of her shattered door, and then back at Ron in disbelief. "Yes," she finally surrendered.

She backed up and let Ron in. She pointed toward the fireplace. "You can put your stuff there," she said.

Ron squeezed around her and set up the chalkboard.

He heard the mumbling behind him slowly settle into silence. He looked into the dozen pairs of expectant eyes. Rather than introduce himself or do anything to break the ice, he launched straight into showing the plan.

Twenty-five minutes later, Ron was sweaty, chalk dust floating in the air around him. "That's it," he told his audience. "What do you think?"

There was a moment of silence as everyone waited for someone else to speak.

"What's the name of it?" a man asked.

Oh, yeah, that. "It's the Amway Corporation," he announced.

Ron stood expectantly for a few more cavernous seconds. It was the first time he was able to truly focus on the people in the room. Ken's brother was asleep on the couch, periodically emitting little snoring noises. Ken was avoiding his wife's steely gaze.

"How about some coffee?" Ken finally announced. "Sarah just brewed a fresh pot in the kitchen," he said, pointing the way.

The room came back to life, and people started making their way to the coffee. Ron followed slowly.

As people enjoyed coffee and snacks, the room fell into friendly chatter. Ron poured coffee for the man standing behind him in line and then filled his own cup. He later learned the man was Ken's best friend, who was also named Ron.

"So, what do you think?" Ron asked Ron.

The man's brow furrowed. Ron braced for a storm. Instead, the man spoke frankly: "I think I understand most of what you were saying, but how do you get your business going?"

Ron was caught off-guard. He'd prepared to answer all the objections, but he wasn't sure what to do with an honest request about how to build a business. He parroted what he'd heard Jim say the weekend before: "Well, next Saturday, host a meeting at your house, one like we had tonight. Ken here will come over and show the plan for you."

Ron's hopes of having made a successful handoff were short-lived. Sarah, who he hadn't realized was standing right behind him, cut in immediately: "No, he won't."

Ron turned around, startled. He nodded to her awkwardly, made an unsuccessful attempt at a smile, and then turned back to the other Ron. He swallowed. "Okay, well then, I will."

After that, Ron never missed holding a Saturday meeting, and the Kuklinskis are still in the business today.

Though I hadn't attended that meeting, in the coming months I heard about the business repeatedly. I was still negative, but Ron was working so hard that it was getting more difficult to root against him. At the same time, I wasn't about to let him know I was slipping into his corner.

> *I was still negative, but Ron was working so hard that it was getting more difficult to root against him.*

Ron knew the value of personal reviews, so he left some of the product under the sink, hoping I'd use it and like it. I wouldn't touch the stuff. I just kept using the products I bought from the supermarket, the ones I had always used. When I didn't get the hint, he tried a more direct approach: "I was wondering if you'd try some of the products, so I can tell people how you like them."

I still wouldn't budge. (I mentioned earlier that I have some of my dad's ornery German in me, didn't I?)

A few Saturdays later, I came home to find that all the cleaning supplies in the house had been removed and replaced with Amway products.

"Where did all my cleaning stuff go?" I asked.

"We have cleaning stuff," Ron answered without looking up from his newspaper.

"No, *my* cleaning stuff. Not Amway stuff."

"Oh," he said causally, "since we didn't need it anymore, I boxed it all up and took it to The Salvation Army. The receipt for taxes is on the desk."

I fumed a little over that, but I finally gave in. Ron was happy as he showed me how to work with the concentrates. I was a little disappointed to see that the Amway stuff worked as well as anything we'd used before. It often worked better. Once Ron told me how much less it cost, I warmed to the idea of using it instead of my store-bought stuff.

Not long after that (about six months after Ron had registered with Amway), he proudly announced, "Okay, Georgia Lee, you don't have to work at Denny's anymore."

> ## 66
> *About six months after Ron had registered with Amway, he proudly announced, "Okay, Georgia Lee, you don't have to work at Denny's anymore."*
> ## 99

"What?" I asked.

"I just looked over our budget. The business is bringing in $400 a month now, basically what you make at Denny's in salary and tips. So there's no need for you to work there anymore. You can stay home with the boys again, just like you always wanted."

I should have shouted for joy. In my heart, that's exactly what I wanted to do, but I didn't want Ron to know he had won. (Oh, how silly our pride can be sometimes!)

I shook my head. "I'm not coming home."

"What?"

"This isn't going to last. I'm not giving up my job, only to ask for it back in a couple of months. I'm not going to quit."

Ron got a little ruffled. "Georgia Lee, I want you home. I'm tired of being the mother on nights and weekends. I'm no good at it. I want you home, and I know you'd rather be home. That is what you want, isn't it?"

I shook my head and didn't say any more. He knew to let it go—for the moment.

He changed tactics. He kept showing me the checks that were coming in. And he waited. He knew I would figure it out for myself.

Of course, I did. It didn't take me long to realize I really didn't want to work anymore if I didn't have to. I didn't like being away from the boys, and I didn't like working late. I didn't like being unavailable for doing things on Saturday. I didn't like *never* having time together as a family—*never* being mom and dad with our kids eating dinner together every night. What was I thinking?

Again, money isn't everything, but it does give you options. It gives you room to think about what you really want out of life and choose *that*, rather than what someone else wants or needs you to do for them. With my salary at Denny's replaced, I could be home or find more fulfilling work. As it turned out, the work I really liked was being a mom.

So I quit.

The first day Ron came home from work and we didn't hand off the keys in the driveway was surreal. Instead I came outside, kissed him on the cheek, and we walked back into the house. It was like we'd just gotten married again. Suddenly we saw a new hope in front of us. The dreams we had as newlyweds started stirring again.

I never did have to ask for my job back at Denny's. Ron kept his word on that.

Ron, meanwhile, continued to put in eighty-hour weeks at the PUD, while also showing the plan one night a week. Not having to work for an income anymore, I started to feel guilty. The least I could do was help. Maybe Amway wasn't so bad after all. It was allowing me to be home with the boys, and I didn't even have to take in other kids to babysit anymore.

One night, I swallowed my pride and asked, "Ron, is there anything I can do to help you with the business?"

He didn't bat an eyelash. "Sure is." He looked me in the eyes, "You could order the products. You could take care of the customers. That would be a big help to me. And you could go out with me when I show the plan."

I told him I would.

"Great!" he said. "And we might as well get started. I've shown the plan to the neighbors who live right over our back fence."

I looked out at our back fence through the patio door.

"They're not interested in the business, but they want to buy some of the products," he continued. "Why don't you take their first order?"

What? I thought. *Right now?*

He knew what my blank stare meant. "Just go over and take their order," he encouraged. "No pressure. They already want to make a purchase."

My forehead creased. "You want me to walk all the way around the block to talk to them?"

He shook his head. "Nah, come on." He handed me a product sample tote tray and motioned toward the patio door.

Curiously, I followed.

We walked to the back fence we shared with the neighbors. He cupped his hands together to make a foothold for me. "Here, I'll boost you over, and you go knock on their back door," he said.

Without really thinking, I stepped into his hands.

"On three. One, two, three—"

I stepped out of his hands. "I can't do this. I'm afraid," I said.

"Sure, you can," he reassured. "You can do this. It's going to be so easy. It's going to be so good." He held out his hands again and I stepped back into them. "One, two, three—"

He lifted me back up on top of the fence.

Losing my confidence again, I fell back down. I told him, "I can't. I can't do this. I'm not ready to do this."

"Oh, sure you are," he said even more confidently than before. "You know the products. You've used most of them yourself. You've heard me share about them dozens of times. If you're not going to do it now, then when? Why wait? It's always good to get the first time out of the way. Now, one, two—"

He never got to "three." He lifted me up and over the fence before I had a chance to react.

I landed rather unceremoniously on the other side, with a thump.

Getting up, I rubbed the grass off of my backside and turned to scold him.

> *Losing my confidence again, I fell back down. I told him, "I can't. I can't do this. I'm not ready to do this."*

"Here," he said, handing me the sample tray.

Once I took it, he turned, walked back to the house, and went inside. He closed the door behind him before I could get a word out. Then he sat and pretended to read a brochure at the table, looking up every few seconds to see what I was doing. When I caught him looking, he smiled. Then he seemed to find something really interesting in the brochure again.

I knew he was right. If I was going to get started in the business, there was no time like the present. I picked the last few blades of grass off of my backside, went up to our neighbor's back door, and knocked.

I sold them two products—SA-8 and LOC—that night. As I walked around the block to return home, I realized I'd just done what I had said I would never do: I'd just sold my first soap. As they say, "Never say never."

When I returned home, I was excited. Ron and I were now in business together.

I have to admit—it felt pretty good.

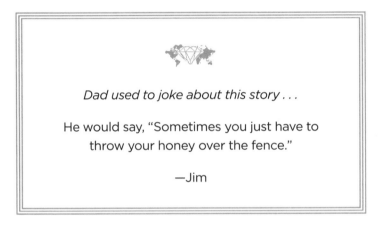

Dad used to joke about this story . . .

He would say, "Sometimes you just have to throw your honey over the fence."

—Jim

POTENTIAL IS GREAT, BUT IT'S GROWTH THAT COUNTS

We weren't overnight wonders in this business. And it wasn't a straight-upward climb to success for us. A lot of times it was two steps forward, three steps back, then another two forward, if you know what I mean. There were plenty of defeats and "no's" along the way to discourage us. Every meeting felt like we were starting over. Despite his determination, Ron felt like he had to re-sponsor himself every day.

In her book, *Mindset: The New Psychology of Success,*[2] Dr. Carol S. Dweck outlines two kinds of mindsets people tend to express when they approach something difficult. The first is what she calls a *fixed mindset*.

> Believing that your qualities are carved in stone—the fixed mindset—creates an urgency to prove yourself over and over. If you have only a certain amount of intelligence, a certain personality, and a certain moral character—well, then you'd better prove that you have a healthy dose of them.[3]

That's because a fixed-mindset person is afraid of being exposed as lacking or insufficient.

But there is a second kind of response, one that's key for a successful entrepreneur. This response

> is based on the belief that your basic qualities are things you can cultivate through your efforts, your strategies, and help from others. Although people may differ in every which way—in their initial talents and aptitudes, interests, or temperaments—everyone can change and grow through application and experience.[4]

Dr. Dweck calls this the *growth mindset*.

Ron and I learned to choose the growth mindset. It didn't take long to see that the more we were willing to change and grow, the more our business grew. The more we stretched ourselves, the more effective we became. Almost nothing was easy. We had to look ourselves in the mirror every day and find the courage to step out of our comfort zone one more time. We needed to do things we weren't good at so that we could get better at them.

If speaking in front of a group scares you so much that it makes you throw up, go ahead and vomit. Then wash out your mouth, slap some water on your face, and go speak. It will get easier, but you'll have to face down a lot of nerves before it does.

Then the challenges will up the ante. Over the years, Ron went from speaking in front of a dozen people to speaking before thousands. It took a while, but he became a sought-after speaker, and there were a lot of "bathroom breaks" before he became comfortable in front of a crowd. That's just how life is if you want to be a meaningful specific. You're going to upset some apple carts along the way, and most of them will be your own.

Honestly, it doesn't get easier, because the challenges you face get bigger. As you grow, the capacity for what you can tackle increases. Some people tell you that you can work this business for a few years and then coast. That wasn't true for Ron and me. The more your business grows, the more people look to you to point the way and help them know how to handle their hardships. The good news is that each step along the way prepares you for the next—but you still have to summon the courage to take the next step and risk falling on your face again—and again, and again.

You have to keep growing and be disciplined in doing your work and showing the plan. Only then will your business help you start capturing your dreams. Ron and I knew that the Lord blesses effort, courage, and faithfulness. As the Good Book says, "As you sow, so shall you reap." You get the harvest you've planted and nurtured. You can't sow laziness and reap diligence. Everything produces after its kind.

Another daily decision is to choose humility over pride. Pride says, "I don't have to grow. I have status. Others should applaud me for who I am and what I've done." Some people don't want to be humble because they think it's groveling. It isn't. Humility says, "I am not any better or worse than anyone else. I can always be better than I am, and I am thankful to God for putting me in positions to learn and for bringing me people to learn from."

You don't have to be something great to think that you *are* something great. It's just human nature to want to be admired and appreciated. No matter who you are, rich or poor, disciplined or undisciplined, the CEO of a company or a temp in the data entry pool, we all want to be regarded as significant. We all want to be important. The foolish look at their current status and try to convince themselves they are already impressive. People should look up to them because they went to the right school, have the right friends, or say the right things. They should be respected because they are good at something, or because they are good-looking, or because they are on the right side of some issue. They matter because they have a nice car or nice clothes. They earn a large salary or boast an impressive title. Such things are the spice of life, but they aren't a good basis for defining who we really are. These things are nice window dressing, not foundational stones like character, integrity, and dependability.

When Ron decided to start an Amway business and sell soap to make a little money on the side, I wanted nothing to do with it. Why? Because I had status. I was a waitress, bringing in just enough money to feed our family. That made me important. I was "too good" to be associated with the guy in the holey T-shirt dragging his wagon full of laundry detergent door to door. I was just fine the way I was.

> *When Ron decided to start an Amway business and sell soap to make a little money on the side, I wanted nothing to do with it. Why? Because I had status.*

Ron felt the same way when Jim first called to discuss a business opportunity with us: "What? You think we need to make a little extra on the side? Don't you know we're doing great? We're glad to have you over, but we don't need a new business. Why don't you come over and let us hear what you've gotten yourself into? Maybe we can find a way to get you back into a rut like we are."

That's what pride will tell you is right. It will rot your thinking and trap you in the world's expectations. It will bury you in debt, doing unfulfilling work with limited opportunity, striving against your coworkers for the next promotion rather than working together to build something everyone will benefit from. Craving status will trap you in a dreamless, visionless lifestyle. You buy things you don't need to impress people who don't care anyway.

> *Humility says . . . I don't need status to believe in myself or feel loved. What I need is a vision big enough to motivate me to endure the pain of growth.*

If you want to live differently, you need to do things differently. You need to overcome your need for status and choose to grow instead.

Humility and pride say different things. Humility says, "This is where I came from. This is who I am because of my background and where I grew up. This is the family I was born into. These will always be part of who I am, but they will not limit who I can become. I have the power to choose to be something more. Who I am today is nothing compared to who I will be tomorrow. I don't need status to believe in myself or feel loved. What I need is a vision big enough to motivate me to endure the pain of growth. I'm going to look at things honestly, assess where I am, and plan how to achieve the future I want for my family and me. It's not about who I am on the outside; it's about who I am becoming on the inside."

Before you go to bed tonight, sit down with your spouse. (If you're single, sit down on your own or with a trusted friend or relative for coffee or something, or just call them on the phone.) Make a list of at least ten things you want for your future. What is really important to you? What are the "status symbols" that are holding you back? You've probably bounced your dreams around in your head in the past. There are things you'd like to have, places you'd like to go, things you'd like to experience. Maybe it's a new home, a new car, a college education for your children, a family vacation to Hawaii, or building a well in a refugee village. You probably know what you want from life, but you've never committed it to writing. Do that tonight.

Next, set goals for yourself. What do you want to accomplish in your business? Where do you need to grow? What do you need to let go of or grow out of? (For example, don't immediately quit your day job and go full-time in the business. Set milestones and replace your income first.)

How much will it take to replace your salary, or your spouse's? Where does your business need to be to supply that much? Once you have answered these questions, set those benchmarks as your first set of goals. Achieve one before you move on to the next and before you step into the lifestyle it will provide.

Every one of us should have a vision for four areas of life: family, career, spiritual growth, and finances. Your vision in those four areas is the goose that lays the golden eggs. That's what will bring blessings into your life. That's where joy comes from, a real sense of identity. That's what makes life worth living.

PRINCIPLE #5

TO EXIST ONLY FOR SELF IS EMPTY.

YOU MUST LIVE FOR AND ASPIRE

TO SOMETHING GREATER

IF YOU WANT TO BUILD A LEGACY

FOR THOSE YOU LOVE.

5

You Need to Live for Something Greater Than Yourself

A handful of weeks after I "got off the fence," Ron approached a coworker at the PUD, someone he thought would be a good prospect for the business. His name was Lonnie. Lonnie thanked Ron for the invitation but said he wasn't interested in starting his own business. Ron wasn't offended. He liked Lonnie. He was a good guy, so he stayed what our son Jim likes to call "sticky." He kept in touch and kept being friendly.

Lonnie and his wife belonged to a nondenominational church in Pasco called Tri-Cities Christian Center. As Ron and Lonnie became better friends, Lonnie invited Ron and me to attend church with him and his wife. This time it was Ron's turn to say no. That went on for a while. Ron would invite Lonnie to a meeting. Lonnie would invite Ron to church. Both always received "no" answers.

As the two became better friends, Lonnie softened. The next time Ron invited him to a meeting, Lonnie made a counteroffer: "If you and Georgia Lee come to church with us, I'll come to one of your meetings."

Ron agreed on the spot.

I grew up going to Sunday school and church camps, but it had always been just for fun. I never really knew what church was about. God was a vague, distant notion to me. I attended church because my friends invited me and I liked being with them. I learned about Jesus and heard Bible stories and did my crafts. None of it affected me much. Ron and I never discussed the idea of attending church as adults. Neither of us had any affinity for religion.

So we had no idea what we were in for.

The churches in Grangeville had all been very traditional and strict. They were all formal and ran like clockwork. What we heard that morning was completely different. The music was contemporary and heartfelt. It moved us both. And we had never heard anyone talk about Jesus like we did that morning. We'd never heard an invitation to accept His forgiveness and ask Him to come into our lives.

That may sound strange if you are not a Christian or have never been to a contemporary evangelical church. It's not my desire to get preachy or tell you what to believe about God or the universe, but something in the message that day really touched our hearts.

Regardless of what you believe, we all know the power of selfishness, how being selfish can hurt those around us. We all know how life's problems can overwhelm us, drive us toward caring only about what we want and doing only what makes us feel better about ourselves. Life can make us self-medicate or insist on doing what we want, without caring how it affects anyone else. The years of living in quiet desperation (as our debts grew and Ron's work life grew more difficult) had taken a toll on our marriage. We still loved each other, but sometimes it didn't feel like it. We'd fallen into patterns of treating each other poorly. Although getting into Amway had relieved some of the financial pressures we faced (and eliminated my need to work outside the home), Ron and I still sometimes clashed horribly over little things, unimportant things. Something was missing in our lives, and we didn't know how to fill the void. The frustration of that unfilled need often made us act selfishly and tore at our relationship and our family.

> *It's not my desire to get preachy or tell you what to believe about God or the universe, but something in the message that day really touched our hearts.*

What we heard that morning promised to fill that void. When the pastor invited us to come forward, accept Jesus into our hearts, and surrender our lives to God, both Ron and I felt certain that's what we needed to do to reclaim our happiness and find our purpose in life.

But that Sunday, neither of us had the courage to step forward.

We saw people walk to the front at the invitation, and I knew, beyond a shadow of a doubt, that I needed to go. But I didn't know what Ron was thinking, and I wanted to know what was going to happen to those people before I joined them.

When I saw that nothing weird happened, I wished I had gone forward, but the service ended, and we filed out with everyone else. Later that day, Ron told me he had wanted to go up too. We could have walked out of church that Sunday morning, hand in hand in the sunshine, having accepted the Lord together. Instead we drove very carefully and wore our seat belts until the following Sunday.

The next Sunday, Ron and I arrived at church in time to sit near the front. At the end of the service, we responded to the pastor's invitation, as a family with the boys in tow. We accepted Jesus as our personal Savior and Lord. It was the best decision we ever made. It made all the difference in our marriage, our family life, and so much else in the years to come.

In becoming Christians, we learned how to please God and be in relationship with Him in everything we did. We learned we could face anything with Him. I don't mean to make it sound pie-in-the-sky. It wasn't like life was a rose garden after that, but it made hardships more bearable because it gave them meaning and purpose. Life took on a greater meaning. So did our business.

Ron and I both wondered what would have happened if we hadn't invited Lonnie to a meeting. Would we have ever have gone to church? We certainly wouldn't have been interested in going if it weren't for our quid pro quo with Lonnie. (And, yes, Lonnie attended a meeting, and we eventually became his sponsors.)

> *Even modern psychologists are finding the value of ancient proverbs and admonitions. Love is still the value and action that conquers all.*

Because the business helped us find Jesus, Ron and I dedicated our Amway business to God, as well as everything else we did in life. Our work with World Wide Dreambuilders also had God at the forefront of our efforts. We dedicated it to God from day one.

We now had one more reason to be grateful for the business—the greatest reason of all.

From that day forward, God would be our partner, and we would always strive to honor Him. We would never force our beliefs on anyone, but we promised ourselves that we would create a safe place to talk about God, to be honest about what He'd done for our lives and our business.

Ron and I felt affirmed, and we learned great lessons at Tri-Cities Christian Center. We started attending Wednesday-night Bible studies whenever we could—whenever we didn't have a business meeting or some other commitment. The senior pastor understood. He encouraged us to be there as much as possible, and he didn't judge us if we had a conflict. The door was always open. That meant a great deal to us, and we've always tried to emulate that spirit in our personal business and in leading World Wide.

LEADING FROM THE BOTTOM

Over the next several years, our Christian faith taught us several things that became central to the founding, growth, and success of World Wide Dreambuilders. It's what taught us the principles of True North. As with many faith traditions, a strong component of being a Christian is to live by wisdom and give of oneself to other people. It's interesting to see the similar core values across different faiths, things like the Golden Rule: "Do unto others as you would have them do unto you."

Today, wisdom has gotten a bad reputation because so many people think it's based on opinion and outdated thinking. It's not. Wisdom is based on an understanding of human nature that comes from centuries of observation and recognizing the true nature of things. There is certainly a divine ingredient, but even modern psychologists are finding the value of ancient proverbs and admonitions. Love is still the value and action that conquers all.

We'd like to think we're smarter than folks were 5,000 years ago, or even 500 years. Objectively we are, but human nature itself hasn't changed. We still struggle with the same wants and desires, the same instincts and weakness, and the same battles between pride and humility. Arrogance still comes before a fall. Lying still undermines trust and destroys relationships. "The more things change, the more they stay the same" is an enduring truth, especially when it comes to human nature. The things that trip us up today are the same things that tripped up Adam and Eve. Only the packaging is different.

Perhaps the most important World Wide wisdom principle is based on something Jesus said: "Anyone wanting to be the greatest must be the least—the servant of all!"[5] We have seen, time and again, those who build the biggest businesses and grow them the fastest are the people who put the needs of their downline before their own. The strongest families in this business are the husbands and wives who put the needs of their spouse first, second only to their dedication to God.

Success comes from putting what is best for others before what is best for ourselves. It's counterintuitive to what most leaders in business do, but even in corporations it's a principle for being great. You don't have to look further than the writings of John C. Maxwell or books like *Good to Great*[6] to see this is true.

The key is submitting to one another in love—putting others' needs before our own.

Submission is a tough topic today because it has been so abused. It has so long been a shoe worn on the wrong foot. Submission was never meant to be a tool for those in charge, a tool to subordinate others. It is better understood as the attitude of someone who wants to grow and succeed. In a successful business, people are so busy submitting to each other—trying to make others successful—that who's in charge is of secondary importance.

Before I push further into this topic, let me clear up a huge misunderstanding. To submit is not to make oneself a doormat for others, nor does it mean we should never stand up against abuse. Submission is not relinquishing our human dignity or letting others treat us poorly. The only people who can truly submit to someone else are those who believe in themselves and have self-confidence. Only people with personal power and ambition truly submit. The powerless cannot. They surrender, and surrender is about as far from submission as you can get.

> " *Success comes from putting what is best for others before what is best for ourselves.* "

The essence of submission is yielding your right of authority to another person. To do that, you must have authority to yield. Surrender is giving up our personal authority altogether. They are different things.

Another principle you see scattered throughout wisdom traditions is that we should "love our neighbors as ourselves." We all seem to value the first part of that and stumble at the second. To love, you must have the strength to love. You must have solid ground beneath your feet to love from. That means you have to love yourself first. You can't help someone by jumping in a hole with them. You must be firmly tethered to something outside of the hole. Then you can throw down a rope and rescue them. If you don't have a firm place to stand—a place where you know you are worthy of love—you will get stuck in the hole too.

The Bible tells us that wives should submit to their husbands.[7] When I first heard that, I had some issues with it. (Maybe this is true of you too.) But before you throw this book out the window, allow me a moment to explain. It isn't just that I have some ornery German blood in me (which I do) or that I think the instruction is sexist. It was hard for me to consider putting *anyone* before myself at that time, let alone my husband. It was something I wasn't mature enough or confident enough to do at that time. I struggled with the thought of submitting to someone else, because, frankly, I had a hard time loving myself. I had little concept of my personal power, let alone of feeling worthwhile as a human being.

Marriages succeed when husbands and wives are *for* each other; *us* needs to be more important than *me*. Families succeed when there is a proper set of priorities for each spouse. For the wife, the husband is more important than the children; for the husband, the wife is more important than anything except God. That means he puts the wife before the kids, before his career or business, and before hanging out with his buddies. All of those things need to submit to the needs of his wife. And the needs related to his job must come second to his family's needs. (That's often hard to do if you work for someone else and have a demanding boss who requires more of your time than is reasonable. That's a boss who has his or her own priorities out of whack.)

> *Submission is not about something the other person should do. It's about what I do because I want to actively love someone.*

Marriages fail when husbands and wives are against each other. When *me* is more important than *us*; when the kids or work or playing golf or anything else is more important than one's spouse. When we are abusive to one another—whether verbally, emotionally, or physically—we are eating away at our own souls. When we think submitting is more for the other person than for ourselves, we're sowing seeds of brokenness and disconnection. Such things tear relationships apart.

Submission is not about something the other person should do. It's about what I do because I want to actively love someone. Submission is the opposite of "Me first."

That sounds great in theory, especially when both spouses are in full agreement, but what about the disagreements? How does it work in practice? What about Saturday night when you are tired and want to curl up on the couch and watch a movie, but your spouse is telling you to get dressed because you are scheduled to go show the plan at someone's house? What about when your spouse hurts your feelings and you want to strike back? What about when someone in your down-line borrows money from you and then disappears? What about when someone is trying to turn you into a doormat, and you know they are in the wrong?

What does submission mean in situations like those? How can you be a "servant of all" when someone is trying to take advantage?

You follow the Golden Rule. If circumstances were reversed, what would you want someone to do to you? Do *that*. Sometimes that will mean saying "no" and offering a more acceptable alternative. Sometimes it will mean being the adult in the room and helping the other person grow. It means doing the best thing for them, even if it's something completely different from what they are proposing.

WWDB is blessed to have Paul and Billie Kaye Tsika in our lives. Paul is our pastor/spiritual advisor and spends untold hours doing exactly that: pastoring and advising and counseling. Paul and Billie Kaye wrote the book *Get Married, Stay Married*, which I encourage you to get and read. Do they know what they are talking about? Yes! Most definitely.

The spiritual part of your life helps you understand what is really important, because it helps you know you matter to the universe. It gives you a place to stand, from which you can love and help others. People without a spiritual foundation tend to feel like they need to justify themselves all of the time. Their identity gets wrapped up in what they do and have done, rather than who they are becoming. They live for others to notice them, to see them as significant. They feel a need to distinguish themselves from others, and this often expresses itself in a constant rebellion against everything around them. I don't mean a rebellion against injustice or corruption—which should be rebelled against—but a rebellion against authority and wisdom in general. Some people always need to be the center of attention, so they want to do everything differently so that they stick out from the crowd. It's not a bad instinct. We all have it. But knowing who you are on the inside gives you the strength to lift other people rather than lifting yourself.

Being in submission (being humble) isn't playing it small. It's not standing in the corner, being a wallflower, and going along with whatever everyone else wants, without having an opinion, without questioning something you think is wrong. Submission doesn't mean always agreeing with others, always giving in to what they want, or biting your tongue when you think they're about to make a mistake. It means you want the best for them as well as for yourself. So, if you see or hear something suspicious, say something, but say it in a kind way so people can accept it. Of course, you should listen before you speak. Make sure you understand someone's perspective before you disagree with him or her. You are a cheerleader for your team, and you are a thinker, part of the brain trust that makes your business work.

Be heard. Express your reservations or ideas. However, don't get your nose out of joint if you don't get your way. You're working together for success, and mistakes will be made. You are as likely to be wrong as your partner. Being part of a real team means you don't have to say, "I told you so." Be supportive, help evaluate mistakes, and be part of the solution to move forward smarter in the future.

Again, it all goes back to *choosing* to be happy, and we believe that happiness comes from doing things God's way, acting according to long-standing wisdom.

Ron and I believed that when God gives a command, He's not trying to control you. He's giving advice about the best way to live. He, the Designer, is telling you how you were designed to be happy. He's telling you that if you do such-and-such, it will

> *Be heard. Express your reservations or ideas. However, don't get your nose out of joint if you don't get your way.*

benefit you. Otherwise, as life goes on, it will hurt you. It's a little like telling your kids not to touch a hot stove. "Is that a rule?" they might ask.

"Well, not exactly. It's just that it will really hurt if you do it, and I don't want you to be hurt."

"So, if it's not a rule, then I can choose to touch it if I want?"

"No, I wouldn't say that. You could choose to touch it, but you won't like the consequences."

"So if I choose to touch it, you're going to punish me?"

"No, if you choose to touch it, you're going to punish yourself."

"You're just making that up to control me. I don't believe you."

"No, I love you, and I want you to be happy. I don't want you to be hurt."

"So, if I choose to touch it, it's my fault I get hurt?"

"Well, yes, but it's better if you don't touch it. That way, you won't be hurt. But you could choose to do other than I say and burn your finger. You will be sorry you did. Then you're not likely to make the same mistake again, but I'd rather you listened to reason and learned from wisdom, rather than learning through being hurt."

The Bible is full of this kind of wisdom, and we rebel against that wisdom at our own peril. But we don't follow this teaching just because we think it's good advice; we've also proven it out. Following the Bible's teachings has brought us success in our family and our business. We truly believe that it has made World Wide what it is today.

That's where our strength is. If you look at our organization and see good fruit, that's where it comes from. We didn't come up with a bunch of original ideas that we thought sounded good to build our business on. We sought out what made others successful, and we made their methods our own. Those decisions made all the difference for us. They will do the same for you.

You may believe a little differently than we do, but it is our belief to put God first, respect those in your family, and respect those you do business with. Those are values we hold as self-evident. We can work out the rest. We are in this together. World Wide was created to make every member successful and happy. Help us help you do that.

PRINCIPLE #6

EMPLOYEES SHOW UP AND DO WHAT
IS REQUIRED OF THEM.

OWNERS TAKE RESPONSIBILITY FOR
REALIZING THEIR DREAMS.

SUCCESSFUL LEADERS UNDERSTAND
THE PURPOSES, SYSTEMS, AND
RELATIONSHIPS OF THE WHOLE.

6

It's a Business, Not a J-O-B

While me joining Ron in the business made things better for us, it certainly didn't vault us to overnight success. Gains in this business tend to be small ones that gather momentum over time. Little decisions in the present can have big impact down the road—for good or for ill. That's why it's wise to stay teachable and open to change. It's good to stay willing to turn on a dime—it can keep you from running into a wall.

With the two of us building the business, we could divide the labor. I took over all ordering and product delivery. (I became our shipping and handling department.) Ron stayed focused on sharing the plan and finding prospects. Together, we decided to double our efforts and dedicate two nights a week to sharing the plan, rather than just one.

At first, we ordered product from a Direct Distributor Platinum in town and then picked it up from them. Though they weren't part of our upline, they were familiar with distributing product, and it was easy for them to add our orders to theirs. They had a sizable inventory, so Ron and I would go there with the boys once a week to pick up what people had ordered from us. As soon as I got the hang of it, I'd go on my own with the boys while Ron was at work. We'd load our customers' orders into the station wagon and take them home to divide into individual packages for delivery.

> *Every Sunday night, I would gather all the orders I needed to process and then sit at our dining room table into the wee hours of Monday morning to complete the process.*

As our business grew and our volume increased, we applied for a warehouse authorization so we could order directly from the corporation in Ada, Michigan. There wasn't even telephone ordering back then, let alone anything close to the online ordering we enjoy today. Every Sunday night, I would gather all the orders I needed to process and then sit at our dining room table into the wee hours of Monday morning to complete the process. Everything had to be listed in numerical order and totaled properly so there was no confusion. Once I organized and double-checked everything, I'd complete the order form and write a check. Then Ron would mail it from work the next morning.

It usually took about two weeks to receive our orders. They would come to a freight company in Pasco (across the Columbia River from

Kennewick). While Ron was at work, I went to the freight company to pick them up. I remember the freight guys sitting there, watching me load everything into the Rambler. (They weren't authorized to remove product from the dock, so even if they wanted to help, they couldn't.) Until the boys were older, I did all of the loading. Some of those boxes weighed fifty pounds, but I managed to handle them.

Because the Rambler was our only vehicle, it wasn't long before I started making two trips to get everything home. (Eventually we bought an old, dumpy, beaten-up pickup truck with a stick shift so I could get more product to our garage in one trip.) I can't tell you how many times I drove back and forth between that freight company and our home in that first year, let alone in the years to follow.

Once I got everything back to the garage, I broke it down into individual orders for mailing. There were no UPS or FedEx home pickups back then, so I took those boxes to wherever they would be shipped from. I'd deliver them myself if the destinations were close enough. Some of our personally sponsored distributors picked up their product from our house. We had a two-hour pickup window every week. We shipped a lot of our packages by bus in those days, so I always had a load to drop off at the bus depot. I did this until we were doing 70,000 to 80,000 PV worth of product monthly. Thankfully, that's when Amway was able to start shipping product directly to our home instead of to the freight company. I can't tell you how much time that saved me! (We are so lucky to have that all done at Amway and shipped directly today!)

Despite the growth and the rewards we were receiving from the business, Ron was still nervous every time he shared the plan. Ken Kuklinski once confided to me, "By the second meeting [that we organized], we were tired of waiting for Ron to get out of the bathroom where he'd be throwing up, so I thanked him and showed my own plans."

As you probably know, one of the keys to this business is finding more people to show the business to in a setting that is inviting and friendly. We all tend to listen to people we know, like, and trust, and it wasn't long before we ran out of prospects in our immediate circle of friends and acquaintances. That meant we were constantly brainstorming ideas for how to reach other people who might be interested in the product or starting a business.

One time we sent a mailer to every household in Franklin County to see if anyone was interested in hearing about "a new business opportunity." No one responded. That was when we realized there needed to be a personal connection or people wouldn't come. It wasn't enough to let people know we were having a meeting. They needed to be personally invited by someone they had a connection with or 99.99 percent of them wouldn't come. (And, in our experience, the 0.01 percent were not the kind of people we were looking for.)

You can't go out into the street and hand out brochures with your number on it and get people to sign up as customers or business owners. In fact, pushy practices like that gave Amway a bad name in the early years. People would invite folks over for dinner and then spring an Amway presentation on them. One friend told me that he was invited by a college buddy to go out to a dance club. When he showed up at the buddy's house, he ended up in the middle of an Amway presentation. Crazy! You never know what people will come up with next.

We were never interested in fooling people into the business or signing them up without their knowing what it would cost them to succeed. We wanted the cream off the top, not the whole bucket. That meant building rapport and investing in people. It meant being informative and encouraging, but not salesy and pushy. It meant we needed to make friends rather than just planting people into our downline so it looked more substantial than it was. That meant spending more time with people and establishing them, not just seeing how many we could sponsor in a month.

Though the business was growing, we still didn't feel we knew what we were doing. We knew we needed a better road map. If we wanted to build a bigger business, we needed to talk to people who'd built bigger businesses themselves.

To that end (with Jim and Sharon's blessings), we reached out to Pat and Betty Kaufmann and another couple, Bill and Myrna McDonald, who were both upline from Jim and Sharon, to see what we could learn from them. The Kaufmanns graciously came twice to share the business plan at our little, yellow house in Pasco, but with few experienced people in our immediate area, we still felt largely on our own.

Our families weren't supportive. Talking about our business was taboo at holiday gatherings. However, we did hear a lot about our business from family members. One Easter, my mom was in the kitchen with me. Dad was downstairs in the family room. In the middle of preparing break-

> *We knew we needed a better road map. If we wanted to build a bigger business, we needed to talk to people who'd built bigger businesses themselves.*

fast, Mom started expressing her concerns about our business. She was worried (and Dad was even more worried) that we were neglecting our kids. With all those evening meetings, weren't we hiring too many babysitters? Was working so much good for our family?

As she warmed to her subject, I lost it. I started crying. I remember turning to her and saying, "You don't have to approve of what we're doing. We know what we're doing is right, and if you can't be positive, at least in front of the kids, then you probably shouldn't spend another holiday here."

Thankfully, that put an end to the argument, and the kids were never without their grandparents when we could be together. Eventually they even supported us. (Mom started buying SA-8 from me a few months later.) I also heard, years later after Mom had passed away, about an old friend who was complaining to my dad about Ron, and Amway in general. This man worked at our local bank, and my dad warned him, "If I ever hear you talking about my son-in-law and daughter and Amway again, I'm taking every penny of my money out of this bank and taking it down the street." He was too proud to ever say anything like that to us, but when I heard that, I got a big smile from it.

Dad would always say . . .

"Don't eat your seed. Put the margin and bonus
on the first 500 PV back into the business.
Your business should be paying for itself.
Also, build up a cash reserve before you reward
yourself. Dig your well before you are thirsty."

—Jim

The early years of any business will have lean moments. Even with Amway's low entry costs, a lot of the profit needed to go back into the business if it was going to keep growing. With expenses for refreshments at meetings, building up an in-house inventory to meet orders faster, gasoline, replacing my Denny's salary and tips, and the inevitable unexpected expenses, things were tight for a few years.

From the beginning, we committed to each other that the business would pay its own way or we'd get out. That certainly took determination and much creative thinking over the years, but we stuck to it.

That posed its challenges. For one, the Rambler leaked oil, so Ron would park it a couple houses away from any meeting he was holding. That way, he wouldn't leave an oil slick in the driveway. (We celebrated on the day we finally traded up for a better car.)

Because we didn't have the money to buy a chalkboard for presentations, Ron often borrowed the one from Franklin County PUD. Sometimes he invited people to the PUD auditorium for a presentation. (Once, Ron got so focused on drawing perfect circles to show the business organization that he accidentally stepped off the edge of the stage!)

When those options weren't available, Ron used Jim and Brian's chalkboard from their bedroom, complete with letters and pictures of animals around its borders. In one-on-one meetings, Ron would share the plan on a yellow legal pad with a red felt-tip pen. He was constantly going to the store to buy more.

Amway was still very new in the Northwest in the '70s, and all the Diamonds we knew lived east of the Mississippi. Thus, we devoured any training materials Amway gave us. We cherished tapes of talks on the business, given by people with larger organizations back East. In the early days, these were big reel-to-reel tapes. (Cassette tapes and eight-tracks weren't a thing yet.)

The tapes were often copies of copies of copies recorded by someone in the back of an auditorium. We'd have to sit really close, with the volume turned all the way up, to understand what was being said. A lot of these leaders had Southern accents, and we got so used to it that you can hear some drawl in Ron's early talks.

In addition to those reel-to-reels, Amway used to press little "records," flimsy, thin, white vinyl discs they mailed weekly. Ken and Sarah and others we sponsored would visit on Sunday evenings, and we'd listen to the records while we had cookies or donuts. Ken once joked that he'd probably gained fifty pounds in the process!

When cassettes became available, I would set up all the tape recorders I could borrow in our spare bedroom. I'd hit *play* on one recorder and *record* on all the others. (I had to warn the boys not to make a sound!)

Even though we had only the Rambler to drive, we were still technically a two-car family. Ron's old Chevy Corvair Monza lived in the garage, because it didn't run. We jokingly called it "the turd." When Amway came out with Silicone Glaze Car Polish, Ron got an idea. He went into the garage and polished up the Corvair. It looked great! When we hosted a meeting and people wanted to see how good the car polish was, he'd take them out to the garage. "Check out that shine," he'd tell them. Among our friends, the car quickly became known as "the highly polished turd."

I know the difficulties of building a business often don't sound like much when you encounter them on the pages of a book. Every story has its obstacles, right? Often, difficulties and "hair on fire" problems sound like funny anecdotes when you look back on them. (I admit that most of these are pretty funny in hindsight.) It's easy to gloss over the doubts that plagued you, the challenges that consumed your thoughts, the stress, and the constant desire to quit and go back to doing what the rest of the world was doing, because it feels so much safer being "normal."

Ron and I had to constantly keep deciding to proceed with the business. Things never became "routine." The presentations were never easy for Ron, and it would be quite a while before he got comfortable stepping out of his shell. He was always uncomfortable introducing himself to a stranger or facing the blank, critical stares of an unfamiliar group. It always terrified him, but he kept doing it. He knew the only option was sending me back to Denny's and a life where the money ran out before the month did. The only answer was to keep putting one foot in front of the other and moving toward our vision, even though we sometimes felt like we had no idea what to do next. We had to keep the carrot of our dreams constantly before our eyes.

> *The only answer was to keep putting one foot in front of the other and moving toward our vision, even though we sometimes felt like we had no idea what to do next. We had to keep the carrot of our dreams constantly before our eyes.*

Even though we never considered the business as anything but part-time, it continued to grow and bear fruit. Consistent effort will create an exponential effect. By our thirteenth month, we hit Silver Producer and went into Direct Distributor (known today as Platinum) qualification. Our third and last month of qualification was June of 1973, and we hit our target, turned in our orders to our upline, and thought we were good to go.

That's when our first real business trouble started to brew. We'd made the sales, but then we found out someone upline from us was going to hold on to them past the deadline so that we wouldn't qualify. (Because if we qualified, we would pass them in the business, and they didn't want that. They would qualify the next month, but they wanted to hold our orders and qualify together.)

A human shortcoming had stepped in: ego. It was the craziest thing we'd ever heard. We wouldn't have found out, but one of our downline told us the news. He was more fired up about it than we were.

> *We had a choice: We could give in or we could get going. We were suddenly in a fix we didn't know how to escape.*

He told Ron, "I want you to know something; you can count on me and my mother." He had sponsored his mother in the business, and she had eight little old ladies in Sunnyside, Washington, who were in the business with her. He called his mom, and they made a plan. "You sell this much," she told him, "and my team and I will sell *this* much. We're going to get Ron and Georgia Lee Direct! We'll make up the slack. I'll let you know once we're done."

We had a choice: We could give in or we could get going. We were suddenly in a fix we didn't know how to escape. Even with help from this man and his mother, we needed $4,000 more in sales to make up the difference. We had one week to do it.

Ron got one of those twinkles in his eye. Either he'd come up with something fantastic, or everything was about to go topsy-turvy. He looked at me and said, "Georgia Lee, what happens in June every year?"

"I don't know," I said. "Weddings?"

Kathy and Georgia Lee at home in Grangeville.

Ron excelled as a varsity basketball
player at Grangeville High School.

Ron enlisted in the Army in the fall of 1958,
right after high school. He served proudly
through September of 1961.

Ron was stationed in Germany during his enlistment in the Army.

Ron Puryear and Georgia Lee Pfeffer were married Sunday,
November 3, 1963, at Grangeville Methodist Church.

Our first home as newlyweds: a 10' x 55' trailer home.
We shared Ron's Corvair Monza.

This was one week's product order handled out of
the little garage at our Pasco house. We eventually
moved between 70,000 to 80,000 PV monthly.

Time out for a family picture while living in Pasco, Washington.
Our boys were growing quickly, and we had just begun
to build our business.

This photo was taken in the mid-'70s, when Bill Britt
came to do a meeting for the group we were involved
with in Seattle. This photo op with Bill was a thrill for us;
this was before he began to personally mentor us.

We had such love and respect for Amway founders,
Jay Van Andel and Rich DeVos.
This was our Double Diamond Day Celebration
at Amway Corporate Headquarters.

Ken and Sarah Kuklinski, our first sponsored IBOs and first platinums.

On one of many adventures with precious friends
and business associates, Dave and Jan Severn.

Ron with one of the original Emerald Council members, Theron Nelsen.

Bill and Peggy Britt were our very dear mentors,
encouraging and challenging us to dream big.

Traveling to the Winter Olympics
in Lillehammer in 1994 with the Britts.

Sharing a sweet victory moment as new Triple Diamonds
with Bill and Peggy Britt at FED 1995.

Sharing a celebratory kiss with the love of my life, Ron.

Ron loved a good joke and to have fun
with our friends in this business.

Ron as Winston Churchill.

Kathy Camyn was World Wide's first employee,
working there for twenty years.

The home of World Wide
Dreambuilders circa 1993.

The remodeled World Wide Building was
dedicated as the Ron Puryear Building in 2018.

Ron loved a good game of golf.

Peter Island pals.

Ron treasured his friendship
with John Maxwell.

Paul Tsika came into Ron's life as a trusted spiritual advisor
in 2000 and became a close personal friend.

Ron had a knack for seeing things from a different angle.

Ron and Georgia Lee with second generation
Amway Corporation leaders, Doug DeVos and Steve Van Andel.

This photo was taken for an *AMAGRAM* magazine
story in September 1996.

Ron greets the crowd at one
of the many FEDs over the years.

With dear friends John Maxwell
and World Wide's first CEO, Dick Davis.

"Right," he said. "And what do new couples always need?"

I had no idea where he was going with this. "Patience?" I offered.

"No," he almost laughed. "They need cookware for their new homes!"

"Right," I said. I caught myself before I said, "So?"

"And who has a great line of cookware?"

Now I had it. "Amway!" I said.

I don't remember how we did it, but Ron and I obtained the past few weeks of newspapers and started looking through them to find every local June wedding. Once we had a list, we figured out a way to contact someone in each family to see if they'd like to present a nice, new set of cookware to the bride and groom.

It didn't take us long to get all the orders we needed to guarantee we'd qualify. When we did, we called the people above those who were holding up things up and placed our order with them.

We qualified right on time and made our Platinum trip to visit the Amway Headquarters a few weeks later. It was the first time I had been on an airplane. I remember grabbing Ron's hand as we taxied to the runway. I asked, "Honey, can't we just go the whole way like this?"

We toured the manufacturing plant, met with corporate executives, and received further training in building our business.

Our little side business was becoming an increasingly significant part of our lives.

"OWNING" YOUR BUSINESS

This business is composed, for the most part, of the relationships you have in it and the systems you use to stay organized and build toward your goals. That may sound simple, but if you don't go about it with the right mindset, there's more than enough to overwhelm you along the way.

You need to adjust to the fact that you're no longer just an employee; you're now in charge of every aspect of your business. You're not just a boss; you're the owner. Best-selling author Zig Ziglar explained it this way:

> Several years ago on an extremely hot day, a crew of men were working on the road bed of the railroad when they were interrupted by a slow moving train. The train ground to a stop and a window in the last car—which incidentally was custom made and air conditioned—was raised. A booming, friendly voice called out, "Dave, is that you?" Dave Anderson, the crew chief called back, "Sure is, Jim, and it's really good to see you." With that pleasant exchange, Dave Anderson was invited to join Jim Murphy, the president of the railroad, for a visit. For over an hour the men exchanged pleasantries and then shook hands warmly as the train pulled out.
>
> Dave Anderson's crew immediately surrounded him and to a man expressed astonishment that he knew Jim Murphy, the president of the railroad as a personal friend. Dave then explained that over twenty years earlier he and Jim Murphy had started to work for the railroad on the same day. One of the men, half jokingly and half seriously asked Dave why he was still working out in the hot sun and Jim Murphy had gotten to be president. Rather wistfully Dave explained, "Twenty-three years ago I went to work for $1.75 an hour and Jim Murphy went to work for the railroad."[8]

Employees (and even supervisors) tend to place limits on their responsibilities. It's expressed perfectly in the phrase, "That's not my job." When you work for someone else, you are part of a team. You are responsible for doing your part well, integrating your efforts with those of others, and/or ensuring that those who report to you do their parts correctly. If there's a problem, you can't always be part of solving it. If there's something that needs to be done that's not in your job description, it can be risky to step out and do it, no matter how much you'd like to take responsibility and be a problem solver. Your priorities are given to you by those above you on the organizational chart. Rarely are you responsible for everything. Rarely do you hold complete authority to fix something that isn't working right.

Dad would always say . . .

"Some people make excuses, and
some people make money.
The only difference is the way they think."

—Jim

If you're an owner, however, you can't think like that. Your mottoes need to be, "If it is to be, it is up to me," and "The buck stops here." If a goal isn't met, you can't blame someone else. You can never say, "That's not my job." (Well, you can, but you probably won't be in business very long.) If a system you're using isn't working, you must find a better one. If you're falling short on a goal, you must figure out how to make up the difference.

All Ron and I wanted in our lives was a decent opportunity that would help us chase our dreams. Work didn't scare us. We were always willing to work hard and be dedicated employees wherever we were hired, from the sawmill to the savings and loan to the finance company to Denny's to the PUD. Just give us the opportunity. We'd learn, we'd grow, and we'd do whatever was necessary to succeed. We just needed an opportunity to get us to where we wanted to go. When the chance to own the opportunity came along, it was natural for us to work as hard for it as we would for our employers. It made us happy.

We were doubly happy when we discovered we could share the Amway opportunity with others and help them chase their dreams as well.

> *You don't fail in this business because of any flaw except an inability to work and grow, or the inability to help and inspire others to do the same. You don't have to create the best new thing. You simply repeat, or duplicate, what others have done.*

This is a business of replication. This business is based on creating volume and then helping others replicate your efforts. We wanted to offer the opportunity given to us to others—then help them succeed, just as we were helped. You don't fail in this business because of any flaw except an inability to work and grow, or the inability to help and inspire others to do the same. You don't have to create the best new thing. You simply repeat, or replicate, what others have done. New prospects need to hear the plan the same way you heard it, and the same way every person in World Wide would share it. That repetition builds confidence that this business is for real and that people can make it work for them. The more we act and communicate as one, the more success everyone in World Wide will enjoy.

We're all on this journey of building our independent businesses *together*. It's a journey *of* success, not *to* success. Success isn't a destination. It's not about the recognition. It's not about the money either. It's not about getting to some magical point where you can retire. It's about staying on the journey, continuing to learn and grow, and never quitting on your dreams. That should be exciting to you. It's the promise of a whole lifetime of adventure and building something worthwhile for your family, community, and world.

If that doesn't get you out of bed every morning, I don't know what will. Stay on the journey! Keep the adventure going! You'll never regret it.

PRINCIPLE #7

THERE IS ALWAYS A HIGHER PEAK

IN BUSINESS AND IN MAKING

A DIFFERENCE IN THE WORLD.

ENJOY YOUR VICTORIES,

BUT THE NEXT DAY YOU NEED

TO HAVE A NEW DREAM TO CHASE

OR YOU'LL STAGNATE.

7

The Second Mountain

We went Ruby (15,000 PV) the same month we celebrated our second year in Amway. The business was becoming a great little side income for us. Our two weekly presentations were bearing fruit. In early 1974, Ron's boss told him, "If you're going to work in this district, you need to live in this district," implying that we needed to move to an area covered by the PUD. So we put a down payment on a little, yellow house across the river in Pasco and moved there. That would have been a financial hardship, if not for the extra cash coming in.

About a year later, we upgraded to a nice colonial home in a better neighborhood—somewhere we thought we could put down roots. (The dreams we once deemed pie-in-the-sky were finally coming true.) Around that same time, Ron purchased a used Lincoln Continental to commute to work. Then, during the summer of 1975, he hired a contractor to put a pool in the backyard.

We were approaching our fifth year in the business. We were debt-free and starting to enjoy the perks of extra income.

Though the business was prospering, we still regarded it as a sideline to our "real" work. Ron enjoyed his job, as demanding as it was. It was his career, after all. I remember not wanting to leave my Denny's job because it gave me status as a good worker and as a breadwinner. Ron had a stronger relationship with his work, plus the added self-esteem boost that came from being relied on and looked up to in the office. However, do such things truly fulfill us? It usually takes something major to urge us to consider this question.

> *Thankfully, God is good at providing wake-up calls.*

Thankfully, God is good at providing such wake-up calls.

For us, the wake-up call started with the contractor taking longer than expected to build the pool. By the time it was ready to use, it was already fall and getting cold. Ron had no intention of letting that pool sit idle until spring, so he turned the heater up to 88 degrees and let it run. The boys loved it. They'd run, shivering, to the pool and jump in. Icicles would form in their hair. We were all in la-la land. It was great—for about a month.

Then it came time to pay the piper. Our next utility bill was through the roof—over $800. It was normally about $50. Not realizing the reason for the increase, I was upset. It had to be a mistake. So I called the PUD to complain. The guy told me, "Well, that's no mistake, ma'am. That's what your electric bill is for this month."

That was the first domino. As it turned out, we were in a drought, which affected the amount of water running through the local hydroelectric dams. Less water flow meant lower energy production, so the PUD had launched a major campaign, asking people to conserve electricity. Posters were everywhere at Ron's work.

The guy I spoke to on the phone apparently joked about my call to his boss: "Go figure—Ron Puryear is heating up all of the Tri-Cities and running up an $800 electric bill!"

That raised some eyebrows.

When word got back to Ron, he told me to pay the bill and say no more about it. Then we covered the pool for the winter.

In the midst of this, Ron's boss had told the United Way that the PUD would help with their campaign to raise money from Tri-Cities businesses. His idea of helping was to volunteer Ron to do the work in his free time. Of course, Ron didn't have any free time, so he procrastinated. As the end of the fund-raising drive drew closer (and Ron's boss kept asking him how it was going), he asked one of our downline and me to help him. The downline had quit his job when he went Direct, so he had more free time. We agreed to help where we could.

This Direct was always a bit of a character who had no qualms about being flamboyant. He drove up to Ron's offices in his Cadillac for a meeting. He walked straight into Ron's office like a dart into a bull's-eye. That caused more of a stir than our $800 electric bill.

When Ron's boss saw him, he asked his secretary, "Who's that guy?"

"Oh, that's Ron's buddy," she answered.

The boss grew hot under the collar: "Where does he work?"

"Oh, he doesn't work. The only thing he does now is his Amway business. "

Ron's boss was skeptical. He asked around until he found out where the Direct had worked, and then questioned the Direct's former boss about it. He must've told Ron's boss something along the lines of "He built a big Amway business and just came in one day and quit." Whatever it was the guy told him, it just seemed to make things worse.

Dad and I talked about this a lot . . .

And we would laugh at the reactions of the different people involved. From the secretary's assumption that anyone who did not work for somebody else had to be a "millionaire" to the reaction of his boss being challenged by the kind of car somebody else drove—the two-dimensional, cartoonish images people have of things never ceases to amaze me. I am always curious why people say things like, "Oh, they got lucky and hit it big," instead of "They worked their tail off and built something great."

—Jim

Ron's boss had never thought much of Amway to begin with, and he didn't like some guy who'd made a lot of money at it traipsing around his offices. He wasn't going to stand for it.

When he returned, he summoned Ron to his office.

"Are you doing Amway too?" he greeted Ron. "Is that why you have that Lincoln you park next to my car all the time?" (Ron's boss drove a VW Bug.)

Ron swallowed. He couldn't lie. "Yes, sir," he said. "We sell Amway products a night or two a week after I get done with work."

Ron's boss didn't receive this well. He made it clear he didn't like the idea of his salaried employees having outside jobs. He couldn't fire Ron for doing Amway. There was nothing illegal or unethical about it. It had never interfered with Ron's job. His boss, however, made it pretty clear that Ron needed to either give up Amway or find another day job.

Ron blanched. He didn't know what to do.

He came home, told me what had happened, and we discussed it. "Georgia Lee," he told me, "we're making twice as much with Amway as I am at work. I can't afford to give up Amway. I guess I've got to find another job."

"Okay," I told him.

So Ron resigned the next day. Then he filed for unemployment and started looking for another position. It never occurred to us to do anything different from what we had done before: work Amway on the side while Ron worked as an accountant. After all, what would Ron do if he didn't go to an office every day?

> " *Ron's boss made it pretty clear that Ron needed to either give up Amway or find another day job.* "

To make matters worse, Ron's boss fought Ron's right to get unemployment, to the point there was a hearing about it. He claimed Ron had left for reasons other than what qualified for unemployment. The Direct who'd been helping out with the charity drive served as a witness for Ron, which caused even more friction. Ron's boss did not like the Direct at all, but he was well-spoken and impressive on the stand. Ron got his unemployment benefits and kept looking for another job.

If you know your history, you'll remember there was a recession happening in the mid-1970s. Ron was serious about finding a new job, but there were no open doors in the local area. He was either over- or underqualified. But he kept trying, until his unemployment ran out.

When it did, Ron and I sat down at the base of one of the trees in our front yard to discuss our future. It was a beautiful, crisp winter day. The sun was shining bright. Ron told me, "Georgia Lee, I don't know what we're going to do. There are no more unemployment checks. I can't get a job. How are we going to pay our bills?"

As I thought about this, I had a brain wave. "Well," I suggested, "why don't we treat Amway like a full-time job? We're making this much money working one or two nights a week. What could we do if we worked it full-time? How much could we make if we worked four or five nights a week?"

> "Well," I suggested, "why don't we treat Amway like a full-time job?"

Ron looked at me, considering it. "I don't know," he said. "I've never met anybody who worked it that hard. What would I do during the day?"

"Sleep?" I shrugged. "Do what you want to do. If you're replacing your income, why should you have to go into an office where your boss thinks he should run your life? Let's build the business stronger and harder than we've ever done and see where that takes us."

Ron was a little shocked. "Really? You wouldn't be mad?"

"Why would I be mad?"

Ron's forehead crinkled. "Okay, then," he said, warming to the idea. "What can it hurt to give it a try? It beats going to all these interviews for jobs they don't want to give me."

We sat down and crafted a plan. We would start sharing our business four or five nights a week and see what we could accomplish.

As it turned out, Ron never went for another job interview.

GOING PRO

In the next two and a half years, while working four to six nights a week, Ron and I went from Ruby to Pearl (three Silver Producers or above in one month), running 80,000-plus PV per month, and on to Diamond (breaking nine Direct/Platinum legs within six months of each other). Those years separated us from almost everyone else we'd ever met in Amway.

These events marked another time of divine intervention in our lives. Before that, we were just humming along, playing it small, and growing little by little. We were nowhere near realizing our potential, and we had no dream bigger than getting out of debt, having decent cars, owning a home, and raising our little family. It was sort of like the prayer, "Lord, bless us four—and no more." We thought that was being godly. We didn't want to ask for too much from life.

We needed a serious shake-up.

Once again, blessing came disguised as adversity.

Adversity will come to all of us. Struggle is a part of life, especially if you want to do anything significant and leave your mark on the world. That's a fact. Life's a struggle.

But struggle doesn't have to be negative. You have a choice. You can choose to ignore everything in this book and confront struggle face-first—and it can mow you down. You can struggle but still get further behind in accomplishing your dreams. You might even tell yourself, "Those World Wide folks are crazy! This is too hard! It can't be done unless you luck into the right circumstances. Those people have no idea what it's like to live in my world!"

It's easy to think like that, but if you do, you'll probably get beaten up and eventually quit on your dreams. Most people do. Nothing I've written in this book can be done without resolve, a good deal of effort, and the right attitude. You need an active imagination and a desire to learn. When struggle knocks you down, you need to go to the folks in your upline, listen to another tape, read another book, go to another meeting, reach out to the next person, sell a product, or work more— whatever it takes to get you back on track.

If you do that—if you accept by faith that you have what it takes to overcome the struggles you're facing—then you'll be amazed at what you can accomplish. Instead of struggling negatively and fruitlessly, you can struggle positively.

There's a big difference between struggling negatively and struggling positively. The positive struggle is life. That's what is exciting, because you get to see change in yourself and what you do. You get to bear fruit. You get to see things happen. You get to love the thrill of overcoming. You get to enjoy following the path of an overcomer.

As you consider the year ahead, which will you choose? What is your struggle going to look like? Please give faith a chance. Give it a year. Ron and I believe that God will prove Himself faithful. The struggle must be met with faith. If you'll struggle positively for a year, you'll be amazed at what you can become. It sure beats getting stuck in the rut world like so many do. They'll struggle during the coming year too, but at the end they'll have little or nothing to show for it.

When you have adversity in your life, as we did when Ron's boss gave him that ultimatum, you should be excited, because something new is going to happen. Change is in the air. Is it something that's going to happen to you, or an opportunity you're going to seize?

It's not the struggle that matters; it's whether you keep dreaming in the midst of it. If you struggle while chasing a dream, it is easier to be happy. That's the promise of the free-enterprise system: If you dream it, turn that dream into a vision, and work hard at it, outside of some huge, unexpected tragedy, nothing can stop you from accomplishing your dreams. You can accomplish a little or a lot. It depends on your efforts, intelligence, and willingness to learn. Choosing to struggle positively is the stuff of a successful life.

"What is a successful life?" you might ask. A successful life is progressing toward worthwhile goals. "What is a worthwhile goal?" It's something that makes the world a better place. The more good it produces, the more worthwhile it is.

"So, then, what's a dream?"

> *It's not the struggle that matters; it's whether you keep dreaming in the midst of it. If you struggle while chasing a dream, it is easier to be happy.*

Dreams are rewards that enrich your life and the lives of those you love.

God's laws of success are based on living according to godly priorities and loving and serving others before yourself. So, I encourage you:

1. We believe it is important to live to please God above all else. Make Him number one in all things.

2. If you are married, make your wife or husband number two. Make her or him the most important human in your life—not your children, not your boss, not your buddies, not your mother-in-law, not your parents, not your upline, but your spouse. You should care about your spouse's happiness more than your own.

3. Third are your children. Raise them correctly, and build a home together. Teach your kids to cultivate their dreams, respect their elders, cooperate with others, work hard, and seek wisdom. Teach them to follow your example in serving those around them.

4. Next comes investing in your career or business and making it successful. It is about making and mastering money. Money is part of the engine that fuels your dreams and maintains your lifestyle, but it's less important than the people around you. Money merely allows you to minister to the world, to contribute to others. It's the result of value you create for others.

5. Next, be a contributing citizen in your country and community. As Americans, Ron and I have always considered these United States of America as a gift from God. Many have paid the price for our freedom. We should never take it lightly. We should give back to America and help to keep it great.

6. Then, and only then, come your personal happiness and enjoyment.

Ron and I believe that God should be foremost over everything else in our lives. What we have chosen as a career should never interfere with God's laws.

How did we keep God first? We obeyed Him. We obeyed His laws. We thought about what would please Him rather than doing what would please us. We believed that God's laws said we were to be long-term thinkers and to have patience and let Him have His time in working His will in our lives. We had faith that if we did what He said, He would keep His promises. We had to get rid of the instant-gratification addiction that is so prevalent in our world. We chose to play for keeps. We believed that God is all about playing the long game. It's better to be successful for a dozen tomorrows than to do something that will bring success only for today.

Another critical choice is how to relate to money. Ron and I paid attention to Jesus's warning that we will either serve God or serve money—that we couldn't do both. We learned to depend on God more than on our next paycheck. That's tough for most people to do. Instead of working for money, make it work for you. Free up one of you to be the parent who can be at home whenever your kids come home after school. I know that sounds a little old-fashioned, but the importance of having a parent home for the kids has been lost. Kids need to have interaction with their parents. I believe we do our kids a disservice if we aren't there for them and leave their care to someone else—or worse, just leave them to television and video games until we can get home.

> *It's better to be successful for a dozen tomorrows than to do something that will bring success only for today.*

Kids need parents, preferably two of them. Babysitters can't do the work of a parent. They're not that invested. I was so happy when I finally got to spend the best years of Jim's and Brian's childhoods being their mom. I know not every mom wants to be at home (or can be at home), but it was a blessing to me. I still cherish those years. And things got even better when Ron came home to join me.

Before both parents are home, however, you need to become debt-free. God said, "Owe no one anything, except to love each other."[9] Why? Because He knows what happens to people when they face financial pressure. It's one of the greatest destroyers of families and lives. It makes people lose sight of their dreams, settling for living hand to mouth. It makes people look at tomorrow more than next year, or ten years into the future. Debt creates a mindset that leads to irrational short-term decisions. That's why Romans 13:8 says not to owe anyone anything but to love them. If we don't owe anyone anything, we'll never have to break His laws out of weakness. You can stand tall. Whether you choose Amway as your career or not, I strongly recommend being debt-free. It has given me so much peace of mind.

Next, focus on allowing both spouses to work the business from home. Working together as a married couple brings tremendous power. It was a far cry from the sixteen-hour-a-day "divorce" Ron and I endured when we were both working for someone else.

Think of what you could do if you didn't have to go to an office forty, fifty, or eighty hours a week, at the beck and call of someone else. Ron got to do all kinds of fun things with the boys because he was home. There are so many things good people can do to bloom and blossom personally, while also giving back to their communities. Our country would benefit greatly from godly people with the time to serve in their communities. Successful people who choose to be good patriots and volunteer their time can really make a difference. They can save lives. So having both spouses free to run their business and give back is a great goal. It's also a great step toward realizing your dreams, because every dream needs time as well as money to make it happen.

> *Successful people who choose to be good patriots and volunteer their time can really make a difference. They can save lives.*

The next thing to develop is financial security, and then financial independence.

This kind of independence doesn't mean you stop working your business, but it does afford you time and money to be able to do greater things in your life. If you manage your business correctly, it will yield money that can provide for your family and your family's families, as God directs in the book of Proverbs: "A good man leaves an inheritance to his children's children."[10]

In my version of the free-enterprise system, it's God first, people second, and government third. I believe that documents like the Declaration of Independence were intended to preserve and protect a vertical alignment in our nation: "In God we trust." For me, this is the basis of freedom and free enterprise, because government doesn't have to regulate moral people being a blessing to their communities and nation. That's only for those who put themselves first and above God. Living life with the wrong priorities causes problems for everyone.

I like how Helen Steiner Rice put it in her poem "God-given Drive":

> There's a difference between drive and driven,
> The one is selfish, the other God-given,
> For the driven man has but one goal—
> Just worldly wealth and not riches of soul . . .
> And daily he's spurred on to reach and attain
> A higher position, more profit and gain.
> Ambition and wealth become his great needs
> As daily he's driven by avarice and greed . . .
> But most blessed are they who use their drive
> To work with zeal so all men may survive,
> For while they forfeit great personal gain,
> Their work and their zeal are never in vain
> For they contribute to the whole human race,
> And we cannot survive without growing in grace . . .
> So help us, dear God, to choose between
> The driving forces that rule our routine
> So we may make our purpose and goal
> Not power and wealth but the growth of our souls . . .
> And give us strength and drive and desire

To raise our standards and ethics higher,
So all of us and not just a few
May live on earth as You want us to.[11]

Ron and I needed to have God-given drive, rather than being influenced by the "stuck in a rut" world around us. We need to live for something bigger than ourselves, especially in how we run our businesses. It's certainly my prayer for all of us in World Wide.

PRINCIPLE #8

YOU'RE NOT IN THIS BUSINESS ALONE.

PEOPLE HAVE TRAVELED THIS ROAD

BEFORE AND HOLD THE KEYS

OF SUCCESS. LEARN FROM THEM.

8

Wisdom Comes from Experience

W hen a business starts to grow, the way you do everything will be tested. Organizing four to six weekly meetings is much harder than organizing one or two. Coordinating the efforts of and educating one hundred folks downline looks a lot different than staying in touch with a dozen. We began to see the value of having a support system focused solely on providing training and motivational materials to people we sponsored. That way, we could focus on connecting with people to become customers and IBOs.

Ron discovered this after talking over coffee one day with a downline leader. He told Ron, "Hey, I've got this group, and they've kind of flattened out."

Ron said, "Yeah, I've got one like that too."

The two thought for a moment, and Ron had an idea. "What if we shook it up? What if you came and spoke to my group, and I worked with yours?"

They agreed and gave it a try. The presence of a new face strengthened the confidence of the downline. It wasn't new material, just a fresh voice. They were surprised at the result. Both groups got a boost from the confirmation of vision and wisdom they had been taught.

Things like this further convinced Ron that we needed a cohesive support system for our downline or our business would stagnate. We needed to ensure we could manage the growth we hoped to see. It's impossible for one person to build a business *and* keep up with all the training and development that's needed as the business's downline takes on growth of its own. Without a system, you can lose people as quickly as you can sponsor others. That's what was happening to us. You can't be everything to everybody. You need help.

Ron took this problem upline, asking if any of them would consider forming a support system that would provide training and motivation as its sole purpose. No one was interested.

In the early '70s, we were introduced to a couple who'd just moved to Seattle who were downline in a large system from the East Coast. They were Emerald Directs, and the husband was looking for some people to create a system, which he would lead. Because we didn't have anything like that, it seemed like a godsend.

The first event with this new group was held in Seattle. The couple invited some Diamonds from back East to speak, and I can't tell you what it meant to have personal access to folks who had built such large businesses. We were a little starry-eyed. They said they would set up meetings like this every three months. We thought we were on our way.

I remember being so impressed with the East Coast Diamonds and how classy they were. (One of the guys wore a leather suit, which I thought was all the rage!) I was intimidated by the wives and their beautiful dresses and jewelry. One of them was a vivacious, giggly, and bubbly speaker. I thought, *Oh, that's what I need to do. I need to be more like her.*

Another speaker was quiet and thoughtful. As I listened to her, I changed my mind: *Oh, I need to be more like* her!

The way these people spoke, the way they dressed, and the confidence with which they carried themselves—it was all too much.

A few months later, yet another successful Diamond lady, with her own unique personality, would be on the stage, giving me *another* person to emulate. And so it went.

This was a new world for Ron and me. It took me years to realize that I could simply be myself and do just fine. There is room for different people. I didn't need to be a cookie-cutter version of the women I saw on

> *It took me years to realize that I could simply be myself and do just fine. . . . I didn't need to be a cookie-cutter version of the women I saw on stage.*

stage. I didn't need to be anyone else, just the best version of myself. I would strive to please God, not all these flashy people. But it took me a while to figure that out.

We soon learned that success isn't only about doing the right things; it's about doing things the right way and for the right reasons. If you get into this business to build your ego more than your business, you're headed for trouble. You must have the heart of a servant or you will have issues with folks; you're going to be offended by what others do or say. People will always be people. Relationships—from your spouse to your up-, down-, and crosslines—will be fraught with conflict and heartache if you have control issues, are overly competitive, act immaturely, or don't give people room to grow.

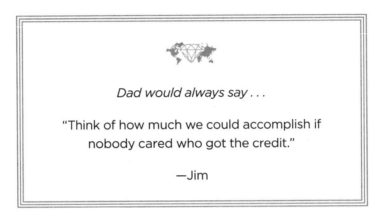

Dad would always say . . .

"Think of how much we could accomplish if nobody cared who got the credit."

—Jim

Little things add up over time.

This is what happened in the system we had joined. Ron and I had big aspirations, and that seemed to make some people uncomfortable with having us around. It took a long time to see this, however, because it began so subtly.

The first hint of trouble was when Ron's questions about growing bigger in any meaningful way were not answered with anything more than platitudes. They never suggested anything specific or practical. It made things uncomfortable, but nothing we couldn't handle. Ron always had very thick skin when it came to how people treated him.

Next, the meetings in Seattle every three months became mandatory if we wanted to stay in the system. That seemed okay at first, until we had to make our first drive to Seattle in a snowstorm! We made it, but when we suggested that we avoid risking people's lives in bad weather, we were accused of not having the drive it took to be successful. That shut us up quickly.

Then there was a ski outing, and everyone but Ron and I were invited. It really hurt my feelings. We were starting to feel more out than in.

Then there was the difference in philosophy about how to build one's business. The leadership of that system taught that you developed two or three legs and then just worked to keep them healthy. That was it. To them, anything more was crazy. Ron determined that wasn't enough for us. We'd developed seven, then eight, and then nine legs. To manage them, Ron made his week ten days instead of seven. He dedicated one night a week to work each leg and then took the Sabbath off.

Dad would always say . . .

"What you do for one, you do for all. By not including everyone, whether you intend to or not, you are telling some that 'you are either not wanted or not important enough to remember.'"

—Jim

We heard through the grapevine that people were being told what we were doing was too intense, that it would eventually implode, and that they should stay away from us. We couldn't believe it. Our business was growing and healthy, so we believed we had proof that what we were doing worked. Rather than clash heads about it, though, Ron chose to be the bigger person for the sake of the overall group. After all, we had to spend time with these folks only every few months, not every day.

Still, I cried every time we headed for Seattle. Then I'd cry all the way home. For good measure, I cried every night while we were in Seattle, because of what I heard they were saying about Ron and how they praised the progress of almost everyone but him. It made me miserable.

Ron tried to comfort me: "Georgia Lee, don't worry about it. I didn't get into this business for recognition. I don't like to speak anyway. They can do anything they want to do to me. But I'll tell you one thing: If they ever try it with any of our downline, I'm going to put my foot down. I don't know what I'm going to do, but I will not allow them to treat our downline the way they treat us."

We remained in that system for roughly five years. Because of what we learned and how much we'd grown, we went Emerald in March of 1978, after almost six and a half years in the business. But our success seemed to make things worse when we went to Seattle for meetings.

> "Hi, Georgia Lee. This is Rich DeVos." All I could get out was, "You've got to be kidding."

Sure enough, we went into Diamond qualification. Those we were coaching started telling us they were feeling uncomfortable at the Seattle meetings. They didn't feel welcome anymore. Ron told me, "We can't continue like this. We have to do something." (This was the impetus for Cardinal Rule #3: "Never embarrass or put down anyone.")

Meanwhile, Amway rewarded us for what we were building. I remember the night I answered the phone and heard, "Hi, Georgia Lee. This is Rich DeVos."

I was floored. All I could get out was, "You've got to be kidding."

"No, really," he responded.

"Oh, no," I said. "You've got to be kidding."

I could almost hear him smiling.

"Really?" I asked.

"Really," he said, half laughing.

I called Ron to get on the other line. Rich said he wanted to congratulate us before we received our Diamond pins in the mail. We were both floored that he took the time to call us. It meant the world to us. Despite our misgivings about the *system* we were in, we knew we were in the right business.

To address the problems in our Seattle-based system, Ron connected with four families: the Daugherys, the Nelsens, Dave and Jo Eggers, and the Hedgecocks. Together we formed what we came to call the "Emerald Council." We gathered at the Sunriver Resort near Bend, Oregon, to discuss ideas and options. Sunriver is a beautiful resort on the eastern slope of the Cascades.

It was a great time to get away. Sharing two houses and parking a couple of RVs close by, we cooked and ate together. We enjoyed the natural beauty. It was a celebration of what we had accomplished in our businesses and a time to chart our way forward.

At one point, Ron told the group, "I have to admit that I've been a fool. We were taking advice from people who, I believe, are leading us down the wrong path. We cannot survive unless we find somebody we can learn from who has built a business like what we want to build. Someone we can trust, someone who will edify what we're doing, not tear it down. We need to find a godly person we can follow, someone who can help us build our businesses to the Diamond level and beyond."

Everyone agreed, so we brainstormed about what to do next. We recalled that our Seattle meetings allowed us to meet some of the "bigger pins" from back East. We thought about Bill and Peggy Britt and wondered if they would take us under their wing. If so, we'd jump at the opportunity. (We had listened to several of their tapes and had heard them speak in Seattle.)

Ron noted, "Next month, the annual convention is in Grand Rapids. I'll go with the sole purpose of finding somebody who's willing to adopt us. I'd like it to be Bill Britt. If any of you want to come with me, that would be great."

So Ron and a couple of the other guys attended the convention at the Grand Rapids Grand Plaza Hotel. It was crazy; there were people everywhere.

After one of the first meetings, Ron stood waiting for an elevator. When the elevator door opened, who should walk out but Bill and Peggy Britt.

They had no idea who Ron was, of course, but Ron wasn't going to miss an opportunity that was obviously God-directed. Ron offered his hand: "Mr. Britt, my name is Ron Puryear, and I have a growing business out in the Pacific Northwest. We just became Diamonds."

Bill shook his hand and congratulated him.

"I have a bit of a situation on my hands," Ron got right to the point. "I'd love to get your insights. I know you're busy and don't have the time to hear all that's going on in my life. After all, you don't even know me. But could I have a few minutes of your time during the convention?"

Bill eyeballed Ron up and down. "It's nice to meet you," he said, "but I'm sorry, I'm busy. I'm on my way to a meeting."

Then he grasped Ron's hand a little longer and looked deeper into his eyes.

"Come with me," he said.

Ron didn't hesitate. He nodded and walked down the hallway with Bill and waited outside the room where Bill had his meeting.

Once Bill's meeting was over, he sat down with Ron and asked to hear what was going on. Ron explained everything as fairly and honestly as he could. "What I'd like to know, sir," Ron concluded, "is if you'd be willing to adopt and mentor our group."

Bill scratched his chin and thought about it.

"Okay," he said. "I might be willing to do that, if you're willing to prove that you're on the up-and-up. I'm going to give you one year. If I hear anything negative or derogatory, I will have nothing more to do with you. If you keep your noses clean and don't cause trouble, I will adopt you."

I can only imagine the smile on Ron's face as he heard this news. I wish I'd been there to see it.

After Ron returned from Grand Rapids, we started organizing our own meetings. Our first World Wide Dreambuilders Family Reunion was held in July of 1979 at the Spokane Convention Center and Opera House. Bill and Peggy spoke, as did another Diamond couple they'd invited from their organization, Britt Worldwide.

> *I can only imagine the smile on Ron's face as he heard this news. I wish I'd been there to see it.*

It was our first meeting on our own, and we filled the Opera House.

Bill and Peggy Britt were absolutely wonderful to us the entire time we knew them. They didn't have any children, so it often felt like we were their kids. We were in seventh heaven under their mentorship. Our future looked bright again.

SEEK WISDOM, AND WITH IT, GET UNDERSTANDING

When Ron spoke about secrets of success, he often told the following story:

There was a young man who wanted to be successful.

He had a burning desire for success, a desire he felt deep in his bones. It consumed his every thought. He was determined to do everything he could to be successful.

In his pursuit, he heard about a wise man who could help him. Many people told him, "If you are serious about being successful, you need to go see the wise man."

"Where do I find him?"

"You must search for him with all of your heart."

For years, the young man looked for clues about this wise man's location. He followed every clue until, one day, he discovered where the wise man lived.

He spared no expense, in both time and money, to visit the wise man.

When he came to the wise man's house, he knocked on the door and entered when beckoned.

"What do you want?" the wise man asked.

"Sir," he asked, "what is the secret to success? I am young and willing to work and learn and grow. I have ambition. I have a dream. What must I learn? What must I do to be successful?"

The wise man looked at him for a few long seconds. Then he turned his back on the young man and walked out a back door into a garden.

Can you imagine what went through that young man's mind? He'd traveled so far for this? To be ignored? All his hopes seemed dashed in an instant. He felt thoroughly defeated.

But quitters never win, and winners never quit. And this young man had no quit in him.

He followed the wise man into the garden. *No,* he thought, *I'm going to ask him again—and again and again, if necessary—until he gives me an answer.*

He stood before the wise man with both feet planted firmly. He bowed his head and asked, "Sir, why did you turn your back on me? What must I do to learn your secret? Everyone told me I must speak with you. I've gone into debt

> **"** *"Sir," he asked, "what is the secret to success?"* **"**

and devoted time I can't spare to meet you. What must I do for you to answer my question? What is the secret to success?"

With his cold, steel-gray eyes, the wise man looked deeply into the young man's soul.

For a moment, the young man thought he was about to speak.

Again, the wise man walked away.

The young man was beside himself as he watched the old man walk down to the riverbank and stare at the water.

The young man was confused. He couldn't believe what was happening.

He considered giving up again. But he had no other options. He'd backed himself into a corner. He had to learn the secret to success. He had nowhere else to go. He believed that this man's wisdom was the key to achieving his dream.

So, again, he followed. He didn't merely amble along; he ran down to the river. He watched the old man wade out until the water was up to his stomach.

The young man followed and stood before him again. "What do I have to do to be successful?" he asked.

Again, the wise man didn't say a word. Instead, he put his hands on the young man's shoulders. His steely grip was like a vise. Then he pushed the young man under the water.

At first the young man thought it was some kind of cleansing—a ritual baptism of sorts—but then the old man didn't bring him back to the surface. He held him submerged.

The young man tried to push his way back to the surface, but he made no headway. The wise man's grip grew tighter and tighter. The young man became concerned, then worried, then frantic. He began thrashing about and fighting with all of his strength. The tighter the wise man's grip, the more the young man fought. Soon there was nothing in the young man's mind but fighting his way to the surface and taking his next breath of air.

Still the wise man held him, mercilessly.

Then, just as he was sure he would drown, the young man was freed. He came up coughing and gasping for air.

He looked at the wise man, staring daggers. "Why did you do that? What on earth is the matter with you?"

"Young man," the wise man said, "you want the secret to success? I just gave it to you. When you learn to fight for your dream like you just fought for your life, you will never have to worry about whether or not you will succeed."

If you don't seek wisdom first and foremost, you will end up repeating the mistakes of others, mistakes that will waste your time or, perhaps, set you back and cost you severely. Why do that? Why spin your wheels? Why do things others would advise you to avoid, if only you'd ask them? Isn't it better to succeed efficiently rather than stringing things out? That's just common sense.

That's the strength of belonging to a system, of being part of a group like World Wide Dreambuilders. Ron saw that from the beginning. The weaknesses of your small business will be magnified as you grow—unless you grow faster personally than your business does. You can't build a tower that will stand for one hundred years without a stable foundation, nor can you build a Diamondship that will outlive you unless you build it on wisdom and discipline.

To be guided by True North (wisdom), you must account for the pull of magnetic north (ego). If you aren't willing to lay down your ego, you will never be able to get where you want to go, along a true and direct course.

Of course, our businesses are not identical. We operate from different spots on the globe. We express ourselves in different ways. We are all unique. We approach life from different perspectives.

Dad would always say . . .

"Every light attracts its own bugs."

—Jim

Overall, however, sound business principles and systems share common traits, despite their different manifestations. World Wide's Rubies, Emeralds, and Diamonds are different people, but they follow the same principles. They all teach the same thing, but their personalities differ and they use different analogies as they communicate.

Our people say the same things but in different ways. We tend to resonate more with some people than with others, but World Wide follows the same guideposts. Give it two or three years, and you'll start sounding like your favorite Rubies, Emeralds, and Diamonds. Of course, your exact words and your experiences will be unique to you.

The more you stick with it, the more you'll learn to count on your upline. Their success depends on their ability to help you succeed. I prefer to take advice from someone who has an interest in me, who wants my success even more than I want it. Imagine being stuck in the bottom of a well, and the only escape method is to boost somebody else up first. Then he or she can pull you out.

That person must be someone you can trust. That's why we built World Wide: so you would have access to folks like that.

PRINCIPLE #9

CHARACTER IS THE

BEDROCK OF SUCCESS.

PERSONALITY CAN GROW A BUSINESS,

BUT CHARACTER

WILL MAINTAIN IT AND TAKE IT

TO THE NEXT LEVEL.

9

Outer Success Is Built
from Inner Character

———

Stepping away from the Seattle-based system brought immediate challenges. We'd never organized big events or provided instructional materials for large groups of people. We knew we would need experienced help with these tasks. We didn't want to "reinvent the wheel."

Planning a Puryear Family Reunion in Spokane was one thing, but Dave and Jo Eggers were also trying to organize an event at the Ashland Hills Convention Center in Ashland, Oregon, that winter. (Dave and Jo were living in Coos Bay, about 180 miles from Ashland, at the time.)

We planned to follow the calendar used by Britt Worldwide and host Dream Nights early in the year, with follow-up meetings soon after. Each of the Emerald Council husbands—Jack Daughery, Dave Eggers, Greg

Hedgecock, Theron Nelsen, and Ron—spoke at both events. It didn't take long to see that organizing and running these meetings could devour more time than building their businesses.

Dave called Ron. "We should hire somebody to organize the meetings for us," he said. "It's taking too much time away from working our own business." Dave had been thinking of moving to Spokane, because it was a beautiful area with a great airport. It was also a central location for most of the Emerald Council members. Ron and I wanted to return to Spokane, for similar reasons, and because we'd loved living there before. We'd even decided to hold our Family Reunion in Spokane that summer.

> "*What you do for one, you must do for all. It has to be doable for the newest person in the business as well as for the one who's been around the longest.*"

We looked to Bill and Peggy for guidance on setting everything up. I think we overwhelmed them with questions. Bill said that he wanted to deal with only one person and that would be Ron.

Ron resisted. Being in charge was not a major motivator for him. And we had repeatedly seen people trying to manipulate their way into authority through strength of will, personality, and flat-out deception. Ron had no desire to be "the man." He wanted to share leadership equally among everyone on the Emerald Council, but Bill insisted we have one leader.

As Ron would recall later, "When you go through stuff like this, as we did with those in Seattle, you learn what *not* to do, as well as what *to* do. And what not to do can be the more-important lesson. You can't be arbitrary. What you do for one, you must do for all. It has to be doable for the newest person in the business as well as for the one who's been around the longest."

Once Bill endorsed Ron to be the leader, everyone else agreed. Ron became the de facto chairman, but I don't think he ever fully accepted the title, just the responsibility.

I'm biased, but I think Ron was the best choice to lay the groundwork for what would become World Wide. His experience as an accountant and office manager meant he knew how to run a business efficiently and effectively. The system would always remain focused on one goal: meeting the needs of every member so they could build their businesses as painlessly as possible. Our leadership group, the Emerald Council (World Wide's first Management Team) looked at each business's needs and brainstormed ways a central system could support them as they grew. In everything, Bill and Peggy supported us. They loved on us. They backed us up and helped us with functions. They had many successful businesses within their organization, so many of their Diamonds spoke at our meetings. Bill also invited us to his Britt Worldwide events. These were intimidating as heck. Here were Ron and me, these country bumpkins who didn't know anyone other than Bill and Peggy. We wouldn't miss the opportunity, though, because we were hungry to learn and grow. We went, we kept our heads down, and we made new friends.

In the years that followed, Bill and Peggy invited us to vacation with them. Bill was always willing to give Ron his time and share his wisdom. He advised us every step of the way. Ron always credited Bill and Peggy for any success we enjoyed in our own business or in World Wide in general. They became dear, close friends.

During this time, Ron and I and a few others bought a parcel of land on Long Lake, about fifteen miles from Spokane. It was a wonderful place to take the family to swim, go boating, ride dirt bikes, and camp. Because almost everyone within the Emerald Council had RVs, we'd meet there to camp, enjoy the lake and its activities, and then spend time discussing our next steps together. These meetings were a time to get away and be refreshed and to dream together. That plot of land became our "Acres of Diamonds," named after the story about the man who traveled the world looking for success, only to return home and find there were diamonds buried in the lake behind his family house! It was our place to share and develop the ideas that would take us into our own acres of diamonds.

The Emerald Council families were sitting around the campfire at Acres of Diamonds, roasting marshmallows, making s'mores, and doing our best to make each other laugh. As we chatted and joked, the conversation turned to naming our system. The first ideas were the "Puryear Organization" and "Puryear Worldwide," because all the biggest organizations we knew of were named after their founders (Britt Worldwide, the Yager Group, and so on).

Ron vetoed that idea straightaway. This wasn't to be his organization; it belonged to all of us—to every member who signed on. He wanted the name to represent everybody in the organization. Our system was not going to be named after someone; it needed to be something much closer to the DNA of our entire group.

Then someone said, "What about something about building dreams? 'Dream builders' or something like that?"

That resonated. After more discussion, the name "World Wide Dreambuilders" was agreed to by all. WWDB was born. (And, yes, we know that "worldwide" is one word in the dictionary. We wanted to be unconventional.)

We still needed to hire our first employee, someone who was

organized and could manage the "all hands on deck" nature of organizing events and gathering training materials that would be valuable to IBOs. Because my sister, Kathy, lived in Spokane and was one of the most organized people we knew, we believed she could help us build World Wide from the ground up.

Dave and Jo set up a lunch appointment with Kathy to talk about the job. "This is what we need," they told her, describing all of the areas that needed to be systematized. "Would you be interested in doing all that?" they asked.

Kathy was a mortgage officer at a local bank, and she was tired of her job's repetition. This new job would be anything but repetitive. It also offered opportunities to travel throughout the Pacific Northwest, rather than being stuck in an office. She was interested, but didn't want to jump too quickly. She asked for time to think about it.

She went back to work and told one of her coworkers, Mardy Tucker, "These people are offering me a job starting at what I'm making now. It would be about three or four days a week from 9:00 to 3:00, and I would work from their home. What do you think?"

> *"You're absolutely crazy if you don't take it," Mardy told her. "And next time they need somebody, please have them call me!"*

"You're absolutely crazy if you don't take it," Mardy told her. "And next time they need somebody, please have them call me!"

Kathy took the job but stayed at the bank until the end of the year. Her first official day as the first employee of World Wide Dreambuilders was January 1, 1980. (She would remain part of WWDB for more than twenty years.) Kathy worked part-time as a personal assistant to Dave and Jo and devoted the rest of her time to World Wide.

Ron and I moved back to Spokane (back home) the month before Kathy started. The first Dream Nights officially under the World Wide Dreambuilders banner were organized by Kathy and Jo Eggers in early 1980.

> *No matter how tense or hectic things became, Kathy was always kind and jovial. From the beginning, World Wide learned the value of hiring for character over skills.*

I'm proud to say that Kathy set the gold standard for excellence in how World Wide would operate. She balanced budget sheets to the penny and stayed late when needed to dot all the i's and cross all the t's. She understood the mindset and the "heartset" of the business. She was smart, loyal, and always ready to go the extra mile. No matter how tense or hectic things became, she was always kind and jovial. From the beginning, World Wide learned the value of hiring for character over skills. It's easier to learn how to perform a task than it is to have impeccable character and a great attitude while doing it.

Our personal business was also exploding, so Ron and I decided to hire a personal assistant. We asked Kathy if she knew anyone. She pointed us to Mardy, whom we hired soon after we interviewed her. (In the years to come, we hired several others from that bank. I doubt they appreciated us always taking their best employees!)

For the first year and a half, Kathy worked at the Dave and Jo Eggers's home, but there was significant overlap between the things that needed to be done for their business and for World Wide. Soon World Wide needed more of Kathy's time, and it grew hard for her to prioritize duties. It became evident that World Wide needed a person full-time.

We decided Kathy should step away from being personal assistant for Dave and Jo, and we moved the WWDB office into the home she shared with her husband, Jerry. By that time, there was more work than one person could handle, so Kathy and Jerry finished their basement, transforming it into WWDB offices. In 1983, we hired a woman Kathy had previously worked with at the bank named Joyce Uptmor to be Kathy's assistant.

The first CEO of Worldwide was hired in 1982. The position was given to Dick Davis, who, along with his wife, Vickie, were Rubies downline from Ron and me. Ron met Dick when we wanted to build a sports court for the boys at our home. One morning, Dick showed up to give an estimate for the project. Ron met Dick out in our driveway, still wearing his bathrobe. After they chatted about the project, Dick asked him, "Why are you in your bathrobe in the middle of the morning?" Ron told him about Amway in his casual way. We eventually sponsored Dick and Vickie in the business.

Dick built his business to Ruby, and Ron hired him in addition to Mardy. They both worked for us for a time, each taking care of different things, but Dick worked closer with Ron and World Wide. Because of that, it wasn't a great leap when Dick took over the reins of World Wide as its CEO. He proved instrumental in building World Wide into the organization it is today.

When Dick didn't know how to do something, he dug and dug until he figured it out. He had no problem with confrontation and conflict, which was very helpful for Ron, who hated both. Under Ron's direction, Dick handled those hard conversations needed to keep people's businesses on track and noses in joint. Dick and Ron complemented each other's strengths and weakness and made a great team.

World Wide grew organically from there, based on the needs Ron, Dick, Kathy, and the rest of the staff noted as the WWDB businesses grew. They were constantly asking, "In addition to helping organize meetings and sending out training materials, what other services do World Wide IBOs need?"

Ron almost immediately saw that IBOs needed tax professionals who understood how an Amway business functioned. Finding such a person was a struggle every tax season. Ron asked Mardy (who stayed on as our personal assistant until 1992 and then went to work for World Wide), "Do you know a certified public accountant who has character and will take our business seriously?"

"Yeah," Mardy answered. "My brother-in-law. He lives in the Tri-Cities."

Ron spoke with him, and they launched a WWDB subsidiary called Executive Planners Northwest, a CPA firm that specializes in doing taxes for Amway business owners.

Next, to make WWDB events more memorable, we decided to use inspirational audiovisuals at the meetings. We found a professional photographer who was interested in experimenting with this, and he started taking pictures at events, then transforming them into multimedia presentations. He created slide shows, synced with music and narration. It was amazing. We featured these presentations at Dream Nights and other functions, and people really enjoyed them. This led to designing presentations that could be used by anyone in World Wide. This helped us keep things consistent and repeatable. (Ron used to joke that he wanted to make presenting the plan so simple that it could be done by a dog with a note in his mouth. And we would give the dog the note!) That effort developed into World Wide Productions.

Then there was the need for good training materials, like the cassettes and books warehoused in Dave and Jo's garage. The boxes containing these resources had to be opened, organized, and repackaged into individual orders, ready to be sent to IBOs throughout the Northwest. (And, later, beyond.)

We started recording at our events. We made cassettes of the various presentations. We also created brochures and other materials. This effort came to be known as Diamond Publications.

One by one, World Wide took these services off the plates of IBOs so they could focus on building their businesses and taking care of their downline IBOs. We also created Diamond Travel, because having one central travel office saved everyone money. (As the internet made it easy for individuals to book travel, we eventually closed that department.) Even today, at forty years old, World Wide continues to grow and adapt as the needs of IBOs change.

In 1992, Kathy and Jerry started thinking about downsizing their home. Kathy talked with Dick Davis about moving WWDB into its own offices. By the end of the year, they found a former real estate building that had been empty for some time. It was ugly and filled with huge beetles, but they cleaned it up and it became World Wide's headquarters.

Ron was always inclusive. He never treated World Wide like his personal business. It was created for the success of its membership. To him, the members were the true owners. World Wide did everything according to that mindset. That made the difference in turning World Wide into the organization it is today. It was always based on integrity, efficiency, and service.

CHARACTER IS THE BEDROCK OF TRUE SUCCESS

One translation of the Greek philosopher and engineer Archimedes famously says, "Give me a lever long enough and a fulcrum on which to place it, and I will move the world."

In our world, Amway is the lever that makes things happen. However, it's of little significance if we don't have a solid fulcrum to support the lever. Character is our bedrock. It's a firm fulcrum to help us "move the world." Only when we have character will our businesses achieve their true potential. There is no success if we focus only on what we want and what we can get for ourselves. Such things are always temporary and short-lived. Only what we do for others stands.

Dad would always say . . .

"The bigger my island of knowledge becomes, the larger my shore of wonder gets." In other words, the more I learn, the more I realize I don't know.

—Jim

What is success but a journey to grow us into our better selves and leave a legacy? Success is the progressive realization of worthwhile goals. Yes, there are perks for us to enjoy, but the more success we are blessed with, the more we realize it's not really about us.

At first, your dreams will be immediate: Get out of debt, end the need for either spouse to work for someone else, provide for your family, and provide for your future. But as those needs are met, you begin to dream about providing similar freedoms to others.

Beyond that, what legacy do you want to leave when you're gone? These are things we must grow into. That's why success is a journey, not a destination.

Like any journey, you can't see the whole trip from where you start—or from *any* one point along the way. You see a bit at a time. With each plateau, a new vista appears. With each dream achieved, a bigger and better one lies out on the horizon.

With a clear vision of the direction you want to go, you'll be motivated to overcome your challenges. You'll turn the obstacles placed in front of you into stepping-stones. If you've read a story about anyone who's done something worthwhile, you know it's not easy to achieve big dreams. Men and women who have accomplished great things faced adversity after adversity after adversity. That's what separates the successful from the quitters, isn't it? They didn't get knocked down by adversity and let it keep them down. They kept getting back up and going again. They kept overcoming. They didn't go home and have a pity party; they learned from each challenge and grew to meet the next one.

It may sound strange, but I hope you experience adversities in your business, because adversity helps you build the character you need to succeed. You have to develop resilience. You must persevere. That's what helps you help other people when they face the same situations you've overcome. Nothing worthwhile comes easy. You must be a fighter to build your business large enough to fulfill even your smaller dreams. You must be a scrapper, and mentally tough. Separate yourself from the negative world. Wake up and choose success every day. Choose to think right and do right and refuse the negative. Without the bedrock of character beneath your feet, you will have a tough time building anything.

Character gives you the foundation to follow through and work for your dreams. Character encompasses all the other personal traits we talk about, the ones you need to chase your dreams: commitment, positive attitude, hard work, sacrifice, discipline, humility, service to others, motivation, honesty, and so on. The secret to success is not talent, but character. It's not gifts, but discipline. Successful people do things the right way, avoiding the shortcuts that hurt themselves or others. Like anyone who wants to run a marathon, you must put in the work, even when you don't feel like it.

Dad used to describe it this way . . .

"Picture a stallion on top of a hill, raised on its hind feet, muscles rippling. Tremendous power. Tremendous strength. Picture that stallion against a clear, blue sky on a green, grassy knoll. That horse has tremendous potential to charge.

"Now, picture a bit and bridle in that stallion's mouth, connected to reins in the hands of the Master. That's what God means when He speaks of humility. The power of the horse submitted to God, teachable, confident, but obedient to a higher set of principles is humility."

—Jim

Discipline won't come from external encouragement; it comes from inner desire. It comes from repeatedly doing the next hard task. It comes from obedience to schedule, obedience to planning, and obedience to your vision. As Dr. Jack Hyles wrote in his book *Blue Denim and Lace,* "It is obedience to duty, obedience to right and a subconscious doing of that which is supposed to be done. This is character."[12]

It's tough to develop character without humility.

Many people don't understand humility. A lot of people think that word means, "Please, let me be your doormat. Step on me; abuse me. I won't put up a fuss." But, like submission, humility comes from strength, not weakness. For humility to be genuine, you must know your rightful place in the universe and the difference you are called to make. Operate from this foundation. A truly humble person doesn't look to be less, but to be more. Humble people are teachable, ambitious, willing to be accountable to others, and always looking to lift others higher than themselves. Humility is a big part of having a growth mindset.

Real might lies in control and self-discipline. It is a careful hand that does not rip out the tender shoots of human kindness and gentleness along with the weeds of misunderstanding and disagreement. Being humble means we remain thoughtful of others, even while we build businesses capable of influencing the course of nations. Humble men and women carry mercy along with clout. They are not looking to win wars as much as they hope to free hearts to dream.

As Robert H. Schuller wrote in his book *The Be (Happy) Attitudes*:

> The weak are also mighty when they turn their problems into projects, their sorrows into servants, their difficulties into dividends, their obstacles into opportunities, their tragedies into triumphs, their stumbling blocks into stepping-stones. They look upon an interruption as an interesting interlude. They harvest fruit from frustration. They convert enemies into friends. They look upon adversities as adventures.[13]

I've found few better descriptions of those who are successful in World Wide. Let's keep that growing.

PRINCIPLE #10

MIRROR WHAT YOU ADMIRE.

WHAT YOU SOW IN YOUR BUSINESS

AND RELATIONSHIPS

WILL BE MULTIPLIED BACK TO YOU.

10

You Will Reap What
You Sow—*Multiplied*

B y the early 1980s, we knew the keys to building successful
Amway businesses were consistency and the ability to duplicate
what others had done before. Whenever Ron taught another IBO's
group, he saw how synergy abounded when people heard the same
presentations and principles from different leaders. It strengthened
their knowledge base, and it gave them confidence that the information was reliable, and the methods were repeatable.

This was the beginning of "It should be so simple that a dog with
a note in its mouth could do it—and we'll give the dog the note." Each
World Wide presentation was designed to be easily repeatable, and the
principles taught should be easily identifiable. The more consistency, the
less confusion for new folks starting their businesses, the more credibility they had with prospects because bigger businesses were showing
everything the same way they showed it, and the faster those new folks
could get up and running.

A problem we began running into, however, was when people wanted to do their own thing without checking with anyone else first. This created a ripple throughout the line they were part of. This would cause friction, and people would start to question each other's motives. When this happened, it meant someone upline would need to step in to smooth things out and get everyone back on track.

This led to the birth of the first Cardinal Rule: "Never do anything for the first time without checking upline." This was not a control issue, but a success issue. Anything new needed to fit within the overall framework being established or else it was problematic. Organizational wisdom is a strength, after all, not a weakness. When new things are tried with disastrous results, it is understandable that no one wants to have them repeated. Thus, having a policy of checking upline is the best way to protect against such calamities. It is a lot like the "don't touch a hot stove" rule. People shouldn't have to learn painful lessons for themselves.

> *Organizational wisdom is a strength, after all, not a weakness. When new things are tried with disastrous results, it is understandable that no one wants to have them repeated.*

In our family, I always thought of Ron as my upline. Ron was my upline in this business, but he was also my upline in our marriage and family. It wasn't a power issue; it was about unity. If we were truly doing life together, why wouldn't we always make decisions together? Ron presented ideas to me, and I did the same for him. We were always stronger together. I was always better off when I talked through things with Ron before doing them. Making decisions together made our marriage and business strong.

Ron used to teach:

> We can employ three great powers in our business and our lives: the power of the spoken word, the power of submission, and the power of unity. There is no power in rebellion.

> If you want power in your life, it should come from being willing to submit or making yourself accountable to others in word, deed, and relationship.

This rule is neither good nor bad in itself. In the right hands, it can do great good. In the wrong hands, it can do great harm. Over the years, we have witnessed way too many "Little Napoleons"—people who want to build their little "empires" no matter what it cost anyone else—at every level of the business. They sought to use this rule for their own reasons. And they all went about it the same way: by isolating their group and instilling fear in them about talking to anyone upline. They manipulated so they could be in control.

So that is how the Cardinal Rules were born, starting with #1. IBOs need ways to determine what should and shouldn't be done. To further help with this, Ron created three questions to evaluate any new idea suggested by someone in the group (our son Jim calls these "The IBO Bill of Rights"):

1. Is it moral/ethical?

2. Is it legal?

3. Is it duplicatable?

Dad would always say . . .

"The best and safest point of view to take when evaluating anything is an eternal one."

He was without a doubt the most long-term thinker I have ever even heard of. He always had an eye on what the long-term effects would be, and if it was unclear, he would take a "wait and see" approach. He was often criticized for that, not the least by me.

My brother understood and would always tell me, "Relax. You know his first 'no' does not mean 'no.' It just means, 'Let me think about it.'"

There were many times when Dad might not have been able to immediately express exactly what it was that made him uncomfortable with an idea, but there was something in his gut telling him it was a bad idea and he needed some time to chew on it. I am reminded of the book *Blink* by Malcolm Gladwell.

It is sad how those Diamonds who would demand their way right now instead of allowing time for thought and discussion have not only all fallen out of Diamond qualification but are not even in World Wide anymore. It is bad enough for them, but how many people downline did they hurt by insisting on their own way?

—Jim

If it didn't get a "yes" to all three questions, it wouldn't even be considered. Also, just because it got a "yes" to all three did not mean it was a good idea.

Of course, there were still disagreements. We need to be sure our opinions are based on logic and common sense, not ego. It's also easy to grab short-term growth at the expense of long-term success without realizing that's what you're doing.

World Wide was slowly building organizational wisdom that we hoped would help newer IBOs grow faster and save everyone heartache in the future.

In the midst of developing these operational values, WWDB was also establishing its annual calendar of events. These eventually fell into the four "seasons" World Wide recognizes today: Dream Nights, Spring Leadership, Family Reunions, and Free Enterprise Days (FEDs). As these continually improved each year, they grew and became more and more valuable for members.

Even at the very beginning, meetings were well-attended. In December of 1978, Bill Britt came to speak at Eastern Washington University Pavilion in Cheney, Washington. In these pre-internet days, we used phone trees to get the word out, and we mailed mimeographed fliers. The gym was packed that night—more than 1,500 people attended on only two weeks' notice.

From there we grew to WWDB's biggest event, which we held in the Seattle Kingdome about a decade and a half later in 1993. It drew more than 37,000 people. It was an incredible high to have all of those folks in one place, but the event lacked the personal touch that Ron felt was so important for mentoring. The stage was too far away from the audience, and the logistics were too complicated. The overall feel was cold and impersonal. Although it was a tribute to WWDB to have pulled it off, the Management Team decided that smaller events would be the standard for the future. Today, the largest events we sponsor accommodate 12,000 to 15,000 attendees. Even though it means we have to provide more events and might not be as efficient, it better serves the family DNA that is the World Wide way.

Another thing we did from the beginning was to dedicate Sunday mornings during events to an optional, nondenominational service where the good news of Jesus Christ would be shared. World Wide is not a Christian organization, nor do we require anyone to follow Christian teachings to be a member. However, Ron and I wanted to honor God in everything we did. We were always grateful to Him for every success.

> *Ron's attitude was always, "Hey, if we can help you, we will."*

What's more, many attendees were away from their home churches for the weekend, and the venues we booked were always idle. So why not put them to use? We opened these services to anyone who knew about them, attendee of the function or not.

Of course, all this effort didn't insulate us from other bumps, disagreements, and divisions along the way. We learned each of our Cardinal Rules the hard way. Not everyone bought in to our way of running things.

For example, some folks downline of one of our Diamonds took issue with some of his practices. They didn't like the way he wanted to do business, and they felt he'd misrepresented some things to them. This group approached Ron and insisted the Diamond they disagreed with be "kicked out" of World Wide. They didn't come with a problem to be solved, but with an ultimatum. Given Ron's experience with his boss back at the PUD, I knew they would regret giving Ron an ultimatum. People were free to leave World Wide if they chose, but it wasn't part of who we were to kick anyone out. We were family, and you don't toss out your family members. You find a way to work things out.

Ron's attitude was always, "Hey, if we can help you, we will. If you want to go start your system somewhere else—if World Wide has become too big or you feel constrained by it—we'll help you build your own system or join another system." He adopted the same attitude that Bill Britt reflected to us: We didn't have to be part of his organization to be blessed by him. We were always free to do what we thought was best.

That wasn't what this group was interested in, however. They wanted their own way. They told Ron, "Either you throw him out of World Wide or we're leaving."

Ron's response? "Well, I'm not going to throw anyone out of World Wide."

Their response was, essentially, "Yeah, that's what we thought."

Click. They hung up on him.

And that was that. They disappeared from World Wide.

That was our first "split." Unfortunately, it wouldn't be our last (though, thankfully, we've had very few).

This was part of what formed Cardinal Rule #2: "Never pass negativity downline or crossline. Bring challenges upline." If this group of Diamonds would have had the right intentions and brought their challenge upline rather than built up negativity between themselves first, a solution could have been found. When somebody develops a beef with their upline and then starts spreading negativity to support their position, all they do is put doubt into the minds of their downline. This group of Diamonds have all fallen out of Diamond qualification and most of the people downline from them are not even in the business anymore. How many dreams did they steal by wanting their own way? When somebody spreads negativity about their upline to crossline folks, all they are doing, at best, is undermining somebody else's business and, at worst, looking to recruit support for doing something very destructive.

We all have challenges. We all have things we like and don't like. We have pet peeves. But we should all know the difference between gossip and constructive conversations—between bellyaching and seeking to correct a flaw. We should know what is our business and what is not. What's your ultimate goal? Do you want sympathy, to *be* right, or do you want to *do* right and fix the problem? They don't all necessarily go together.

Gossip and bellyaching spread negativity and feed our lower instincts. They tear down. There's no virtue in tearing down. We should edify instead, and that's more likely to happen when we take our challenges upline instead of downline or crossline. Our downline and crossline don't need it and don't want it. It stresses them out because they have issues of their own—and they don't have any power nor incentive to help you solve your challenges. They have their own situations and their own issues that you should be helping them solve. Your upline is the one who is invested in you. They are building their future on helping you.

Anything negative should stop with you. "The buck stops here" is a great motto for all of us. That's a sign of maturity. It's the essence of being a responsible person. Kids fight over small, silly things; adults take on difficult issues without being ruffled. If you struggle to handle the problem, get help from people who can actually help. That's also maturity. You don't ask your lawyer to check your blood pressure. You don't ask your doctor to repair your car. Go to someone who actually knows how to help. Those people are upline somewhere. They believed in you enough to sponsor you into this business in the first place.

Your upline are kind of like your parents: You're their "kid(s)" in this business. They want the best for you, and they have helpful experience that will put things in perspective.

When you take a situation and a challenge upline, that's not a negative. It's simply a "challenge." If it goes downline or crossline, it's negative garbage. I don't care what kind of issue it is; it could be the most painful thing you've ever experienced. Maybe it's something so painful that it's hard to share, but if you go upline, you're way more

> *Anything negative should stop with you. "The buck stops here" is a great motto for all of us. That's a sign of maturity.*

likely to find a solution than if you just spew out complaints. You can also trust the confidentiality of your upline, more than anyone else. Nobody else's ears are going to hear about your challenge, because it's nobody else's business.

In a family context, going downline or crossline with negativity would be like me going to Jim if I felt a little bit grumpy about something Ron did, or going crossline to my sister and dumping a bit of grumpy on her. I have no right. They have their own lives. They have their own challenges and don't need mine.

So I always went to Ron instead. And if Ron and I had a problem, we could go to Bill and Peggy Britt. Or we could go to our Ultimate Upline in prayer, because God was always for us and never against us. Answers always come from above.

Another rule we created amplified that thought—it wasn't just about spreading negativity, but also about making others look bad to make ourselves look better. It just made sense to add Cardinal Rule #3: "Never embarrass or put down anyone."

For me, that meant never embarrassing Ron by how I dressed or behaved. I dressed with decorum, the way Ron's business partner *should* dress. I even considered how I should look when I was just be-boppin' around town. I didn't wear a long, flowing gown to the grocery store, but even when wearing blue jeans and tennis shoes, I dressed as a representative of our business. After all, who knows whom I might run into? It was all part of my efforts to avoid embarrassing Ron or our business by the way I dressed, talked, and behaved. Wherever I go, I represent my God, my family, and our business. When I act or speak, I want to edify others, not tear them down or shame them.

Because of this business, Ron and I were able to be best friends until the day he went home to be with the Lord. Few other businesses allow a husband and wife to work together as partners or allow them to spend so much time together. I always treasured that. But time together isn't so wonderful when we embarrass or hurt each other.

That's the reason for the third rule. It's important for building our businesses and for staying best friends with our spouses while doing it. The business restored to us the love and the respect we had for each other when we got married. That's something worth protecting.

Another aspect of this rule is how humor was used. Over time we have a tendency to try to "jazz up" our presentations and talks to make them feel more our own. Because the nature of our business is duplication—teaching others to do what we are doing over and over again— that means repetition, and it is very easy to fall into the trap of getting "bored" with constantly repeating the same information.

One of the first and easiest ways to combat repetition is to inject some humor. There is nothing wrong with that if it is done with the right spirit. Unfortunately, it is very easy to hurt somebody's feelings if you make them the butt of a joke. There have been relationships damaged in this business because an upline told a joke about a downline, which hurt the downline's feelings. Then, instead of apologizing and never doing it again, the upline simply said, "It's just a joke."

Dad would always say . . .

"If you are going to tell a joke or make a point that requires a negative example, you better make sure you are the joke or the example."

—Jim

Humor at the expense of others is negative motivation. I don't know how to say this any other way than *never* use negative motivation on people. Bosses can get away with it because, for the most part, people can't just walk away from their job. In Amway, however, people own their own businesses and are not required to put up with being treated poorly. While an atmosphere of friendly competition is valuable, it can quickly devolve into one of manipulation and dog-eat-dog combat if the upline starts trying to shame people into doing things or pits people against each other for recognition. At best there may be some very short-term gain by abusing people in this way, but it *will* fall apart in the long run.

It wasn't too long before we formed Cardinal Rule #4: "Never mess with anyone's money."

A long-standing Amway rule states that once you receive bonus money for anyone else, the bonus needs to be paid to them within twenty-four hours. Once you deposited a bonus check, you immediately wrote and delivered bonus checks to your downline. While that was easy enough to understand and important enough to follow, what about other moneymaking opportunities that came your way? What if someone in your downline came into a tough period and needed cash to save their business? What should a person do then? Is it okay to loan them money?

And what about investment opportunities? People shouldn't keep those to themselves, should they?

We soon learned that the best (and only) advice and opportunities we should be sharing as World Wide members were within the context of growing our Amway businesses with the money that was saved on personal use and earned through retail sales *without* borrowing. This self-reliance was vital to an IBO's success. Almost every time this rule was violated, it cost someone dearly.

> *The first nineteen people Ron shared the opportunity with were not interested in building a business, but Ron earned the business of fifteen of them as retail customers. Ron called that a "Legitimized Business."*

We were blessed to have learned this lesson from the very start. The first nineteen people Ron shared the opportunity with were not interested in building a business, but Ron earned the business of fifteen of them as retail customers. That made our business viable. Ron called that a "Legitimized Business"—one that is profitable on its own and is worth duplicating.

Dad would always say . . .

"While it frustrated me in the beginning that nobody seemed to be interested in the opportunity, over time I was thankful."

Then he'd go on to explain that if he had not gotten those first fifteen customers, his business would have required him to put money into it out of the family's budget. He told me that although he would have understood that the business would still work, it would not have been a viable option for him because we did not have the extra cash to do that.

Because of this, he immediately understood that by turning "no's" to the opportunity into customers, his business became a viable opportunity.

He always taught that while personal use can save money that can be used to "bootstrap" your business in the very beginning, to make it a business worth duplicating, you must have customer volume. By having "failure" on the opportunity side but turning that into success on the customer side of his business, Dad built his belief that the Amway Opportunity was a legitimate long-term business.

—Jim

At one point a very large business leader joined an investment group that promised (and, for a time, delivered) big returns on short-term investments. Innocently wanting to spread the wealth, they shared the opportunity with others in their downline. When push came to shove, it turned out that the investment group was really a Ponzi scheme. Several people in the group lost a lot of money. People got very upset, and the authorities got involved. We learned that when you're a leader in a business environment, the rules change. You become even more responsible for outcomes based on advice that you give, not just on moral grounds but on legal grounds as well.

Again, rather than kicking that leader out, Ron worked out a solution. We made a loan to the leader to satisfy the claims against them, and every dime was eventually repaid to us, though it was a long, hard road to win back everyone's trust.

Dad would always say . . .

"Jim, stick to your knitting. We are not a financial advisor, family counselor, spiritual counselor, or whatever. We are Amway Business Counselors. In every other area, we are a friend who can have empathy and share our struggles and what we have learned and point people to resources that can help, but we are not qualified or licensed to give professional advice."

—Jim

Another area of contention is in the area of financial advice. We have always encouraged people to exercise the principle that "a wise man has many counselors," but it seems like that can easily get blown out of proportion. Whenever somebody would ask Ron a question like, "Hey Ron,

I am thinking of doing. . ." he would always answer the same way: "Well, based on what you have told me, I would do. . . . But you are not me and need to make up your own mind. Have you considered . . ." Then he'd ask a series of questions to help them evaluate whatever they were thinking of doing, whether it was making a purchase, changing jobs, or whatever.

Respecting other people's money is a matter of keeping their success a priority by putting them first and serving their needs. That also means believing in them and trusting they are capable enough to get out of their problems without someone else bailing them out. People enter this business with skepticism, with good reason. There are myriad scams out there. World Wide needs to be a safe place where trust is the main currency. We protect that trust, fiercely. It boils down to four things we *do not* do:

> » We *do not* loan each other money (especially down-line loaning money to upline).
>
> » We *do not* do investments with each other (especially upline soliciting downline to make an investment).
>
> » We *do not* solicit for charities (especially upline soliciting downline).
>
> » We *do not* solicit for outside businesses or those of our friends and family.

The Bible tells us, "For where your treasure is, there your heart will be also."[14] We invest in what matters to us. If you want to see what really matters to someone, watch how they spend their money.

Something Bill Britt once said that I never forgot...

Bill had dropped into Spokane to take a look at the River House. Bill, Dad, and I were standing on the balcony outside of the library overlooking the pool. Out of the blue, Bill said, "We are in a business of beginnings. Everything we do and say impacts people's future. From how we meet people, to how we approach them, to how we show them the business, to how we follow up and follow through with them plants seeds that will bear fruit, either good or bad. It is vital that we do things the right way and not plant the seeds of our own destruction."

—Jim Puryear

If we treasure relationships as we should, Cardinal Rule #5 should be self-explanatory: "Do not mess with anyone else's spouse." We do not prey on each other's businesses, marriages, or families in World Wide. We respect the sanctity of marriage. We respect our family and the families of others.

What you sow into the world—good, bad, or indifferent—tends to be what you reap over time. What you teach your group to do—what you model to them through your words and deeds—will be duplicated and be multiplied in your organization. If you are doing the right thing, you're excited about it. You share it wherever you go, and you set an example for others. What you put in will be multiplied back to you. When you're sharing good things and setting high expectations, you are giving others something to aim for.

If you are cutting corners and being stingy and negative, however, you are sowing something completely different. These things will multiply like weeds instead of bearing fruit.

THE SAFETY VALVE:
WHAT TO DO WHEN THERE'S DISAGREEMENT

There have been other splits and other missteps along the way, but World Wide did not merely survive them—we learned very significant lessons from each. While World Wide took blows from these disagreements, we also became stronger and wiser because of them. Our knowledge of the business and our awareness of what people need to reach their goals came together more clearly and soundly because of the difficulties we faced.

Of course, people are going to disagree occasionally just because we're different. It's not always because of bad eggs. That's why we need a way to resolve conflicts peacefully when we have disagreements. It certainly beats the alternative of giving up or walking away. That is why Ron came up with the "Safety Valve."

As Ron taught us, you must protect your relationships within your Line of Sponsorship. If you don't do everything you can to protect your relationship with your upline, it will be difficult for anyone either downline or upline to trust you. If you are disagreeing with the upline person who is mentoring you, you will be uncomfortable around them and begin to avoid them. That does you no good, and it definitely does no good for those downline from you.

If you are having difficulty with your upline, you have the right to immediately invoke Amway's dispute resolution process. However,

Amway recommends (and so does World Wide) that the first thing you should do is talk to your upline about it and try to clear the air. That does not mean you approach them with an "I am right, and you are wrong" attitude. Let them know that what they are teaching you seems to you to be outside of True North and give them a chance to clarify. Perhaps you're misunderstanding their methods. This is a chance for both of you to learn to communicate better.

If you still feel that what they are teaching is not True North, ask them to check with their upline mentor. After that, if you still are not convinced, ask them to set up a time when the three of you (you, your upline, and your upline's mentor) can talk it out. If they refuse to check with their upline or request the meeting, then (and only then) should you call their upline mentor and request a time for all of you to discuss the challenge. If all three of you cannot resolve it, the next upline mentor will get involved.

> *What you sow is up to you. If you want success, sow success into the lives of others.*

That process is followed all the way up the Line of Sponsorship to the Diamond, then their Diamond, and so forth to the top of the leg until all parties are reconciled. If there is still no resolution, the matter can be appealed to the World Wide Group Management Team. If you still feel that what you are being taught is wrong, you can go to Amway and the Independent Business Owners Association International (the IBOAI). The goal is to resolve the issue as close to the misunderstanding as possible, to preserve relationships. Ron patterned this after Matthew 18 in the Bible.

Solutions are found upline, not downline or crossline. Every person who has left WWDB spread negative rumors crossline first, trying to justify themselves and recruit people to go with them. I have always been mystified by those who left with them. Because Amway will not allow you to change your place in the Line of Sponsorship (which means you will never receive a bonus from Amway on anyone outside of that LOS), you should ask yourself why someone would invite you to leave with them.

What you sow is up to you. If you want success, sow success into the lives of others. If you want love, plant love. Edify others in every conversation you have. As the Golden Rule says, "Treat others the way you want to be treated." It is probably the most powerful happiness principle of all.

PRINCIPLE #11

BE A GIVER, NOT A TAKER.

MONEY IS MERELY A TOOL THAT HELPS
MAKE DREAMS POSSIBLE.

DON'T GET TRANSFIXED WITH
A HAMMER WHEN YOU'RE
TRYING TO BUILD A CATHEDRAL.

11

All That Glitters

The August 1995 meeting of the World Wide Dreambuilders' Management Team was significant for two reasons. One was the need to recover from the turmoil of a split, but in the history of World Wide, I think the other was more significant: We legally gave World Wide Dreambuilders over to her Diamonds.

From the beginning, Ron viewed World Wide as belonging to all of the Diamonds. Unfortunately, there was no legal means to do that. Somebody had to own it. With Bill's guidance, that responsibility fell on us. The Diamond leaders had always acted as World Wide's board of directors, and Ron always sought a consensus among them for any actions World Wide took. In 1994, laws allowing for a limited liability corporation (LLC) were adopted in Washington. As soon as Ron learned this news, he crafted a plan to transfer World Wide's ownership to her

Diamonds. As of this meeting, World Wide now legally belonged to her Diamonds—lock, stock, and barrel.

This decision set World Wide apart from all other systems. And, I believe, it is one of the reasons World Wide is one of the largest systems in the world today. In World Wide Dreambuilders, once a leader achieves and maintains Diamond status with their business for at least a year, they may be invited to become an owner of World Wide. To continue as a member of the Management Team, the Diamond's business must stay qualified at that level or above.

At the time, though, a lot of people thought Ron was crazy for taking this step. Even Amway criticized and questioned Ron about it. They seemed to believe it was a recipe for disaster.

But Ron stuck to his guns. Both he and I were so grateful for all that our business had brought us and all that it had done to bless the IBOs downline from us. To us, it always made sense that World Wide shouldn't belong to us. It should belong to all those who had helped build her and used her to spread blessings to others. It was about the freedom to dream big and develop the resources and time to fulfill those dreams. It was about all of us together making our families, nations, and world stronger and better. It was about helping people live the lives God had called them to. I know it made us far happier to be able to give it away than anything we ever received.

TRUE RICHES

Ron and I could always attest that money doesn't make you happy. A lot of people think money's going to make them happy or that some promotion or new pin in this business is going to mean "I have arrived!" I can tell you from experience that no matter how big the check or the pin, that's not what makes you happy. What makes you happy is having a dream and a purpose in your life and knowing, at least this was true for Ron and I, that you're in God's will as you chase to accomplish them. That's what keeps you young. That's what keeps you excited about life.

It's also knowing you're helping other people and that their lives are better for knowing and working with you. There's nothing like the feeling of accomplishing a dream, but do you want to multiply that feeling tenfold? *Help others accomplish theirs.*

Ron and I started out happily married and as poor as two church mice, living in a fifty-five-foot hallway in a vacant lot with a front- and backyard of weeds and rocks. We were as broke as could be, but as happy as could be. Why? We had a dream. We had a dream of family, friends, a home, and doing things we loved. We had no idea how to accomplish those dreams, but that didn't matter. We were off into a life of adventure together, ready to take on the world.

> *What makes you happy is having a dream and a purpose in your life and knowing you're in God's will as you chase to accomplish them.*

Well, the world did its best to crush those dreams and hopes. It wanted us to be the dog wagged by the tail. It wanted us to get further and further in debt, work all our lives for bosses who were unhappy with their own lives and wanting to take that out on us. To be under someone else's thumb, stressed out, and fighting to make ends meet.

Then we found this business and slowly got to a place where we could dream again. The money and wealth we built didn't make us happy. It was the freedom to dream again, and then the freedom to accomplish those dreams. When we achieved those, we had the freedom for God to give us even bigger dreams. Then He taught us how to help others find the freedom to experience the same things. Money is just a tool—an important one, yes, but it's not an end in itself.

Ron used to say, "I've been happy broke, and I've been happy wealthy. I know money has nothing to do with happiness. Happy is knowing you're going somewhere. It's having goals, having a vision for the four areas of your life: family, career, spiritual growth, and finances."

That's why you can never allow anything to frustrate your dreams. God tells us there are two reasons we become frustrated:

1. A double-minded man is unstable in all his ways (James 1:8). You should have only one vision at a time.

2. When people who have a vision do not see a path to achieving it—when seemingly insurmountable obstacles obscure the way.

Our goal in this business is to take frustrated people who come to us and help them. It's our job to help them take their dream and manifest it into a vision. It's our vision to help them conquer the obstacles and achieve their dreams.

As long as you have a dream and a pulse, you have a chance at the life you want. Life is simply a journey of making decisions. Hopefully, you make enough good decisions to be happy. That means refusing to give up on your aspirations or to be distracted by the numbers or accolades that masquerade for success along the way.

The Bible tells us we have a choice: We can serve God or we can serve money. Many people think that means we're not supposed to have money. But I can tell you from experience that you can serve money whether you have it or not. There's no bondage to money like debt. There's no serving money like having to show up at a job (every Monday morning) that steals the joy from your life, because if you don't, your house gets repossessed. Lacking money usually means that you serve it more than if you had it.

Ron and I avoided serving money by making it serve *us*. We put it to work for us to make our dreams happen. Then we put it to work to help make others' dreams come true. To keep money in a subservient role, we needed to have friends and loved ones we could be accountable to. We needed a community of fellow Dreamers to travel the road of life with, people who would share our dreams, struggles, and successes.

Wealth is a responsibility, one that far too many neglect. It can be a powerful force for good or for harm. Handling wealth wisely demands accountability to people who value the same things we do. You must be a giver, not a taker. It's easy to think we know it all and can rest on our laurels. If we're not careful—if we're not accountable to people we love, trust, and respect—wealth can turn from a blessing into a curse. People will turn against one another, hoping to come away with the biggest piece to spend on themselves and their selfish desires.

Accountable people have four qualities. The first is *vulnerability*. Vulnerability means you're capable of being wounded by others. It means you take risks where you are likely to be disappointed and even discouraged. It means you'll take leaps of faith toward accomplishing your dreams, even though you are sometimes utterly disappointed. You'll

> *Lacking money usually means that you serve it more than if you had it. . . . Wealth is a responsibility, one that far too many neglect. It can be a powerful force for good or for harm.*

travel four hours to do a meeting, and no one will show up. You'll offer wise advice, and people will do just the opposite. You'll give the best presentation of your life, but no one will respond. It happens, but if you don't risk such failures, if you're not willing to be vulnerable, then you'll stay closed to success as well. Failure does not define you; it should motivate you. Failures are simply learning opportunities. Learn from them. Do things better next time. Every "no" is just one step closer to the next "yes." Have grace for mistakes, missteps, and setbacks. Stay open, and continue to risk. Keep trying to bless others, even when it hurts. That's the only way to be blessed yourself.

I'm so glad Ron took my initial negativity about this business and used it as fertilizer to grow our business even faster. If he had listened to me, I would have missed the opportunity to raise our boys firsthand, let alone all the other wonderful things we experienced because of this business. I was closed-minded to the opportunity that eventually strengthened our marriage, allowed us to be financially secure, allowed us to take great trips with great friends, leave a legacy for our children and grandchildren, and so much more.

> " *It's better to learn from other people's experience than suffer their same mistakes.* "

Remember what it means to sponsor someone in this business. That's why World Wide exists. Don't get mad at people for failing to see the potential you are offering them when you present this business. Don't get upset with people. You're not there for you; you're there for them. You're there to bless. Give them time. If this business is for them, if they can succeed with it and bless their families, then they'll come around just like I did. Just love on them. Bless them. Stay positive around them. They're not saying "no" to you; they are saying "no" to the opportunity. Don't let it get your ego out of whack. Don't let it make you think you should quit. Look at the people who've succeeded in this business, and keep your eyes on what they're doing, how they keep going and keep wanting to help others get the freedom they have. That's your guiding light.

The second quality of someone who's accountable is *teachability*. Such people are not just willing to learn; they hunger for knowledge. They're quick to hear and slow to justify themselves or their actions. They consider what others say before they speak. They're open to being corrected; they are open to counsel. If they're doing something wrong, they *want* that call from their upline, asking why they did such-and-such before it gets out of control and hurts them. They'd rather learn from other people's experiences than suffer the same mistakes.

You want people whom you respect to ask about what you're doing in your business and help you make course corrections where needed. People who love learning get excited when they hear the voice of their upline on the phone. They can't wait to get their counsel sheet in front of their leaders, to speak with them personally, and to hear the changes they suggest or get a pat on the back for what is going well. They want others to see their fruit, and they want their upline to teach them how to bear more fruit. It doesn't damage their ego or make them defensive. They just say, "Wow! Thanks for telling me. I didn't realize!"

The third quality of an accountable person is *availability*. They're accessible; they're easy to connect with. They let people interrupt what they are doing because they want to see those people blessed. If someone has an emergency and they call at two in the morning, accountable people don't get mad. They pick up that phone and offer help. (That said, don't call at 2:00 AM if it can wait. Make sure it is an honest-to-God emergency.) If someone calls with an emergency like that, you're tired, and it's inconvenient. However, you're there to help, so you answer the phone. You'll visit them if needed. You're available to your family (kids, siblings, or parents), and you should be available to your World Wide family. Put their needs above yours.

The final characteristic of an accountable person is *honesty*. Accountable people are committed to the truth, regardless of how much it hurts. They are willing to admit what is true. They don't spin events to put themselves in the most favorable light. They hate phoniness and falsehood. They hate lying.

For success in this business, you must be accountable to those upline and downline from you. Be willing to be vulnerable, teachable, and available. Treasure honesty. Be a giver, not a taker. Choose to do the right thing, even when others do you wrong. Turn the other cheek, and don't punch back. Be willing to lose some battles, because your bigger vision is to win the war. You don't have to be right all the time, but always be willing to *do* right by others.

Dad would always say . . .

"Jim, don't be dead right.
Pick your battles, and win the war."

—Jim

Be ready to ask questions and be asked difficult questions. And if you don't know, take the time to find the answer.

Ron once closed a meeting with these words, which I think exemplify the life of being a giver, something he always emphasized. The piece is titled "The Paradoxical Commandments," and it was written in 1968 by a student activist (at Harvard University) named Kent M. Keith. Mother Teresa loved the piece so much that she displayed it on a wall of her home for children in Calcutta:

> People are illogical, unreasonable, and self-centered.
> Love them anyway.
>
> If you do good, people will accuse you of selfish ulterior motives.
> Do good anyway.
>
> If you are successful, you will win false friends and true enemies.
> Succeed anyway.
>
> The good you do today will be forgotten tomorrow.
> Do good anyway.
>
> Honesty and frankness make you vulnerable.
> Be honest and frank anyway.
>
> The biggest men and women with the biggest ideas can be shot down by the smallest men and women with the smallest minds.
> Think big anyway.
>
> People favor underdogs but follow only top dogs.
> Fight for a few underdogs anyway.
>
> What you spend years building may be destroyed overnight.
> Build anyway.
>
> People really need help but may attack you if you do help them.
> Help people anyway.
>
> Give the world the best you have and you'll get kicked in the teeth.
> Give the world the best you have anyway.[15]

People need our best. All that glitters isn't gold. What glitters the brightest are the tears in the eyes of people who are grateful for what you've been able to do for them. Never give people anything but your best. In the end, you'll be glad you did.

PRINCIPLE #12

SUCCESSFUL FAMILIES CREATE

A PLACE OF SAFETY AND LEARNING,

WHILE LOVING EACH MEMBER

TOWARD THEIR BEST.

YOUR BUSINESS WILL GROW

IF YOU DO THE SAME FOR YOUR

WWDB FAMILY.

12

Why We Use Family Language

W e've had great adventures and special times together in World Wide's first forty years. Oh, could I tell you stories: Ron hightailing it out of Mexico when we opened up there, because he was afraid he was going to get cornered for a bribe. Mike and Robin Carroll and two other couples convincing Ron to let them skydive into the middle of a Family Reunion picnic to celebrate going Ruby. And there were spectacular trips to Greece and other places with the Britts and some WWDB Diamonds. So many wonderful memories! I hate that I don't have room to include them all. That would require another book!

What makes it all so special is that, from her conception, World Wide was about building a family business. I don't mean building just the Puryear business, though that was the genesis, but building a system that treated every member of it (every IBO couple and individual) as if they were our brothers and sisters, kids and grandkids. There is a family you are born into and a family you choose. World Wide is the family Ron and I chose to add to our own. There's a reason World Wide calls our big summer functions "Family Reunions." That's really what they are.

When we come together for World Wide events, it's a gathering of brothers and sisters, aunts and uncles, parents and cousins. These are more than words. This is the way we help and cheer for one another. It's very tough to find any other group like ours in the entire world.

Why is it like a family? Well, a family provides you with role models. It provides love, support, stability, and security—all the things we need to become successful adults and responsible, contributing citizens of our country. We need role models, because we don't know everything about this business. We have functions so you can be around more-experienced people. We can hear their stories, and we can see what their success looks like. But we also get to know their hearts and learn the principles that helped them build their business. We need to learn the rules they would never violate and the practices that got them where they are. We need loving and merciful discipline to keep us from violating those rules. We need to hear the dreams that made persevering through the tough times worth the blood, sweat, and tears. That's why I agreed to write this book. These things shouldn't be lost. As one generation of World Wide hands the torch to the next, we want you to prosper in ways we never thought possible. We want you to start where we finished, to stand on our shoulders and build an even better tomorrow for our World Wide family and the nations we touch.

We all have the ability to dream. That's what brought us together. We have parent-child relationships in this business: The "parents" brought us in; the children are those who joined us. Those children grow up and have "children" of their own by bringing new people into our Amway family. And as a parent, what do you want for your children? You want great success for them, don't you? You want them to do more than make money; you want them to be sincerely happy and fulfilled. You want them to develop the personal traits that are most important.

If you picture your Amway business like a family, you'll be successful. If you can love and serve your downline like your children, if you'll be patient with them like you're patient with your kids, they will mature and prosper. If you'll let

> *If you picture your Amway business like a family, you'll be successful.*

them grow into the business and have room and time to mature (and love them rather than judge them), you will experience growth and success. If you will encourage their positive traits and be patient with their shortcomings, Ron and I believe that God will use you in mighty ways. You'll reach your potential and help others reach theirs. For Ron and I, it was the greatest gift we could ever give back to God.

There's much to learn when you enter this business. There's a lot of growth needed and a lot of change to embrace before you realize your dreams. That's done best in a secure and loving environment—one where you trust those you work with and are willing to help them when they need you (just as they've had *your* back). That's what family does. This is what you'll remember on those nights when someone laughs at you or you get a no-show or you're hesitant to answer the phone. This is what will keep you tying one more knot at the end of your rope to hang on to and saying, "I can do this."

When you learn to look at your downline the way you look at your blood family, treat them the same way, and want success for them even more than they want it, you can take your eyes off of yourself and focus on your "kids." When you do that, unforeseen blessings will be on their way.

Like a parent, you have a dual role. You must create your unique plan for your family's success but also reflect the wisdom of your parents.

> **" Ron and I didn't really do these things. We were never that smart. The credit and the glory must go to God, who guided and taught us. "**

You must balance when to speak into your kids' lives and when to listen to them. When to help them course-correct and when to let them make their own decisions (and mistakes). When to comfort them and when to tell them, "Knock that stuff off. Let's get back to accomplishing your dreams!"

What does managing that balance produce? It produces harmony and unity, which feed productivity. That's what produces great fruit.

If you do those things well, then, just as children emulate their parents' success, the people you sponsor will prosper. Your downline "kids" might just go Platinum, and Amway will recognize them as leaders of their own Platinum businesses. They assume more responsibility, and you can inspire more growth.

When people thank me for everything Ron and I have done, when they share a story of something Ron did for them (something that changed their lives or gave them a laugh), I appreciate that so much. It's special. At the same time, Ron and I didn't really do these things. We were never that smart. The credit and the glory must go to God, who guided and taught us.

In chasing after God, we were fortunate to be a conduit of blessing to others. If not for His goodness, grace, and sovereignty over everything we've walked through—some of it great and some of it lousy—we wouldn't have accomplished anything. We would never have built our business or World Wide. There's nothing special about us. God guided us into these principles and practices. We were smart enough to follow Him. Our strength always came from our Lord and Savior.

I hope and pray you can find that for yourself and be the person Ron and I believe God put you on the earth to be. There is no greater accomplishment or happiness.

THE FOUR FOUNDATIONS

In closing, I want to review some foundational principles and practices Ron always pointed to when teaching people how to grow their businesses.

Foundation One: *Never do less than CORE, and do more when you can.* Exercise the Ten CORE Habits (see Appendix B for a refresher course) on a daily and weekly basis. Be consistently CORE. Do that for a full year before you make any big decisions about this business, because the discipline of being CORE will teach you what you can accomplish. Let being CORE lead you to the dream you entered this business to accomplish. Once you've done that, you'll know where to go next. It will be the first hilltop in your journey, the first opportunity for you to see the possibilities ahead with greater perspective.

Foundation Two: *Submit to godly priorities.* Pay attention to what is truly important as you build your business, marriage, family, finances, spiritual life, and so on. Be balanced. You're the source of your own motivation, so make sure you have a dream big enough to motivate you to stick to your priorities and do right by others.

Foundation Three: *Keep the Five Cardinal Rules.* If you break these, you destroy your credibility. Never violate them. The bigger you get in the business, the more important these rules become. Don't expect people to do more than you are willing to do. You should be willing to do more than they expect. They should never feel that you don't have their best interests at heart. The Bible tells us, those "who teach will be judged with greater strictness."[16] In other words, leaders are held to a higher standard.

Foundation Four: *Stay on True North.* Follow wisdom, not your own way. Don't let your ego distract you from your true course. Keep the faith. Turn your dreams into a vision.

There's never a prize without a struggle. I hope you listen when others in the business share the struggles they've experienced. Don't listen only when they talk about the rewards. Compare the struggles you're facing with what they've been through, and know that you can make it too. Be encouraged to conquer the mountain you must climb—just as they did. If you have a vision, then you'll go through the struggle and not quit halfway up the mountain. You'll be able to discipline yourself to get through the hard times because you envision what you'll find on the other side.

When I look back on Ron's and my life together, I see how facing adversity caused us to grow. Each challenge was a stepping-stone to something bigger and better. Each closed door was an opportunity to look for one we could open, to something closer to our dreams. If you search for such doors with a positive attitude, you will find them. The Bible says, "Keep knocking, and the door will be opened to you."[17] Hopefully, you'll look back and thank God that adversity closed certain doors that you would've settled for. That's the way life is. Each roadblock gives you an opportunity to reevaluate your dream and how you're going to fulfill it. If you're open, it will take you to a better path, and you'll be better off in the long run. When you view setbacks with the right attitude, your vision will conquer your circumstances.

> *I know Ron would say this with me: Grow into your goals. Follow your dreams. Let this business bless you beyond anything Ron and I experienced from it. God has big plans for you.*

But what happens when your vision becomes a reality, once you reach your goals? Enjoy it—for a day. Celebrate! Then use the success as a launching pad to your next dream. Keep on the trail of success. Set your sights on something that will keep you growing and working toward accomplishing more. That is the stuff of life.

I know Ron would say this with me: Grow into your goals. Follow your dreams. Let this business bless you beyond anything Ron and I experienced from it. We believe that God has big plans for you. Know that your World Wide family has your back, and that the love you experience here will help sustain you in life.

I can't wait to see what you accomplish.

THE TWELVE

Principle #1:
Your past doesn't determine your future. Your ability
to dream and your willingness to grow and work will lay
the foundation for the business and life you want.

Principle #2:
Every adversity holds a seed of a greater benefit.
When adversity closes one door of opportunity,
are you willing to push open a better one?

Principle #3:
A dream is a destination. A vision is your road map for getting
there. Your dream will perish if it never becomes a vision.

Principle #4:
Don't settle for potential; fulfill it. Grow into the person
who can accomplish your dream; then find a bigger dream
to keep you moving forward.

Principle #5:
To exist only for self is empty. You must live for and
aspire to something greater if you want to build a legacy
for those you love.

Principle #6:
Employees show up and do what is required of them.
Owners take responsibility for realizing their dreams.
Successful leaders understand the purposes, systems,
and relationships of the whole.

PRINCIPLES

Principle #7:
There is always a higher peak in business and in making a difference in the world. Enjoy your victories, but the next day you need to have a new dream to chase or you'll stagnate.

Principle #8:
You're not in this business alone. People have traveled this road before and hold the keys of success. Learn from them.

Principle #9:
Character is the bedrock of success. Personality can grow a business, but character will maintain it and take it to the next level.

Principle #10:
Mirror what you admire. What you sow in your business and relationships will be multiplied back to you.

Principle #11:
Be a giver, not a taker. Money is merely a tool that helps make dreams possible. Don't get transfixed with a hammer when you're trying to build a cathedral.

Principle #12:
Successful families create a place of safety and learning, while loving each member toward their best. Your business will grow if you do the same for your WWDB family.

Appendix A:
The Ideal Business

BY RON PURYEAR

The most important lesson I've learned comes from something
Freud said. He said, "Thinking is rehearsing." What Freud meant
was that thinking is no substitute for acting. In this world, in
investing, in any field, there is no substitute for taking action.[18]

—RICHARD RUSSELL

The following is excerpted from a presentation at
Spring Leadership 2012: audio # WW651.

I ran across this many, many years ago. It's from one of Richard
Russell's *Dow Theory Letters*—dated September 8, 1977. He's discussing the question: What would be the ideal business? He didn't
know what it was. He was just theorizing. In his opinion, there was
no such business—at least not yet.

So, let's measure the Amway business opportunity against Mr.
Russell's theory of the ideal business. He details eleven perfect points
for this "ideal" business.

The first point: If you're going to have a business, you need one that
sells the world. Let's see how Amway stacks up to that. Russell writes,
The ideal business sells the world, rather than a single neighborhood,
city, or locality. In other words, it has a huge market.

Well, Amway is in eighty-five countries and territories throughout the world. Is that big enough for you? Yeah, that's pretty big. That means your potential is virtually unlimited. There's no ceiling.

Amway doesn't say, "Well, you can grow only so big, and then we won't care if you do more. We're not going to pay you any more for doing any more." Instead, Amway says, "Hey, here's a nice safe bottom. If you get in and you're unsatisfied, we'll refund your money." When you sign up, you've risked virtually nothing. Anybody can get in, even people as broke and busy as Georgia Lee and I were. If we can get in and make it work, you can too.

That's one of the great things about Amway. I don't know of another business that operates this way. Amway established a floor, and they removed the ceiling! Amway tells you, "We're not going to limit you. Your only limit is how big you can dream. How many people are you willing to serve? How many people are you willing to help succeed? That's your limit." They don't decide that; that's self-imposed. So, Amway stacks up well against that first point; don't you agree?

Now to the second point: The ideal business has a product with inelastic demand. This means that people need it almost regardless of price.

At first, I didn't know what that meant. I had to look it up in the dictionary. Do you know what *inelastic* means? It means it's a product people need even in a bad economy—not a luxury item like a Mercedes or something. Luxuries sell well in good economies; soap sells regardless of how Wall Street is doing. That means there's an *inelastic demand* for it.

And Amway doesn't just sell soap. Amway has hundreds of unique products and guarantees all of them for 180 days. That should give you enough time to know whether you like it or not. Nobody else can offer that, folks. And they're mostly items folks need every day—they're part of their regular grocery lists. You can't go buy a box of laundry soap, for example, down at the store, use half the box, and then say, "I really don't like this. I want my money back." They'd laugh at you. Not Amway. They'd give your money back. That is pretty unbelievable.

When you think about having a business with so much product support, you should be proud to be part of it. You should be proud of our brands. Home-care products that are the best on the market. They get consistently good reviews from independent sources and have even won awards for excellence. We were organic before organic was cool. We have personal-care products you can't buy anywhere else. Amway

> *You ought to be shouting from the rooftop, "I've found the ideal business! I found the perfect business!"*

has 750 patents on items nobody can get, other than through us. That's pretty awesome, folks, when you think about it.

I don't know why anybody would be ashamed to tell people about Amway. You ought to be shouting from the rooftop, "I've found the ideal business! I found the perfect business!" But if you don't believe it yourself, you can't tell people about it with any kind of conviction.

To be successful at this business, you simply start the process and move up the levels of leadership. When I heard John Maxwell talking about moving up to being a level five leader,[19] I was thinking about Word Wide Dreambuilders. We do exactly what Maxwell was teaching. It's exactly how we teach you. It's exactly what we did to get where we are today. We started the process and never quit, and we invested in ourselves. We bet on ourselves instead of on our job or on our boss.

I remember people telling me at the beginning of our business, "What makes you think that thing's going to last?" My mother cried almost every night because her son, the only one who graduated from high school, was now "jobless," selling Amway. I'd attended business school and had an office job with a title. I wore a shirt and tie every day. She was so proud of me. But when she found out I had gotten into Amway, she wouldn't even buy the product. I'd give her a product and then visit her later, only to find her box of SA-8 still sitting there full. I asked, "Why aren't you using this, Mom?"

> *We bet on ourselves instead of on our job or on our boss.*

"I tried it," she told me. "It eats holes in your clothes."

I said, "Well, how much did you put in?"

But she hadn't even tried it. She didn't want the products to be good, because she didn't want me to stay in Amway. She wanted me to go back to my nice, safe, comfortable desk job and be happy. She worked nights in a cannery—that's cold, hard, miserable work—so she thought I was nuts to give up something with a regular salary and some status. She wanted me to quit dreaming stupid dreams. To her, that's what gets you in trouble. Just be happy with what you've got. "You've got so much more than your dad and I had," she'd say. "Why throw that all away?"

You must be careful who you let speak into your life. Some of the people you love and respect the most can be the most discouraging. If they're not living the lifestyle you want to live, then love them and respect them, but don't take advice from them. You need to take advice from the people who have the lifestyle you want.

With Amway you can own your own business and build it from the ground up, and you don't have to find thousands of dollars in seed money.

But I should move on to point number three: The perfect or ideal business has low labor requirements. The fewer people needed, the better. How many people did you have to hire to start your Amway business? Zero, right? Starting an Amway business is really just "sweat equity." We bought our first house on sweat equity. What's that? That's when you don't have any money up-front, but you agree to fix the place up instead of paying rent. You have to invest the labor but not any overhead.

Now, on to number four: The ideal or perfect business sells a product that has a continuing need. That means it's consumable and necessary. People use it up and then buy it again and again and again. That's what makes the circles work. That's the genius of the plan. That's what Rich DeVos and Jay Van Andel saw when they started this business. Rich DeVos and Jay Van Andel will go down in the history books as two of the world's most influential men. They're going to be right up there with the other level five leaders John Maxwell talks about. Their dream was so big that it included the dreams of the whole world. That's a big dream. Those two guys are special people whom the world should be grateful to. Consumable products are the foundation of Amway. They're not fads that go out of style. They're everyday products people can't do without.

How does Amway stack up on Russell's fourth requirement? Pretty well, don't you think?

On to number five: The ideal business has low overhead. It does not need an expensive location. It does not need large amounts of electricity, advertising, legal advice, and so on. Since we sell their product, Amway takes care of everything that has to do with manufacturing, and they don't charge us. Any other business has to take care of itself, but we don't. Amway takes care of that, so we don't have any overhead.

Now, number six: The ideal business produces a product that is difficult or almost impossible for a competitor to copy. This means the product is an original or requires very special know-how or is protected by copyright and patent. How does Amway stack up here? We have 450 products, with 750 patents on them. You can't get these products anywhere else. We stack up pretty good on that one, right?

Let's go on to number seven: The ideal business does not require huge cash expenditures or large investments in equipment. In other words, it does not tie up your money. We paid twenty-nine dollars for our kit forty years ago. I had to borrow the money to get in, folks. That's how broke we were. And I've never had to borrow a dime to take that twenty-nine-dollar kit and turn it into a Founder's Crownship. We invested our profits back into our business, and we also saved money for personal use. That's a pretty amazing business, isn't it?

Amway is a business anybody can do. It takes away our excuses: "I don't have money." "I don't have time." If you've been listening today, you've learned that many busy people made this business a priority. You've seen example after example right on this stage. They were busy. Everybody's busy. It's not a matter of whether you have the time or money. It's a matter of priorities. What's important to you? Is it following your dreams or watching TV? We all have downtime, nonproductive time. What are you doing with it?

You make a living from eight to five, but you build a life from six to midnight. You must understand that all you'll ever do in an eight-to-five job is make a living. You will be under the control of time and money your whole life. If you want to have a life, though—an adventure, a life of no regrets—what you do with your "nonproductive" time from six to midnight can make that happen.

Amway easily fits into that time, and you can start slowly. You don't have to go at it four or five nights a week. Nobody keeps a time clock on your Amway business. You are your own boss. You establish your schedule as you see fit. And I don't care how busy you are, you can fit Amway into your schedule—into your six to midnight—one or two nights a week. You won't if it's not a priority. That's up to you.

Number eight: The ideal business has cash billings. It's a cash business. It does not tie up your money. That's exactly what Amway is. You probably have some "anyway money" you could be using to build your business. Do what Georgia Lee and I did. We were betting on ourselves. During our first few years, we reinvested our profits in ourselves and the business. This business doesn't require you to handle your accounts receivable. You don't have to borrow money from the bank. You don't have to borrow money from your relatives, and you don't have to find investors. Many businesses require that, but not this one. Just use the product and show the plan. Then sponsor the ones who want to be sponsored, and

> *You make a living from eight to five, but you build a life from six to midnight.*

turn the others into retail clients. Make your first circle work, and then go duplicate it. It's hard for people to tell you it doesn't work when you can show them that it does. Do you think you could do that?

You have the whole world to work with, and I'll help you. You have the support of World Wide and your upline. You have Amway backing you up. You're their only reason for existence. There's nothing to it but to do it and keep doing it. One of the first things the new president of

Amway did was call a meeting to talk to all department heads, managers, VPs—all of them—to say, "The first thing we're going to do is take our organizational chart and flip it around where it belongs. Amway and our leadership are on the bottom. We're down here. The IBOs are up here. I want you to realize that none of you would have a job if it wasn't for them. They're your customers. That's who we serve." Now that's quite a corporation, isn't it? That's a $10.9 billion corporation,[*] and their number-one priority is serving you as an Independent Business Owner. Folks, I don't know who wouldn't be proud to be connected with a company like this.

> *What happens when you watch a movie you really like? . . . You can't wait to tell your friends, "Man, I saw the greatest movie!" Well, why don't you say, "Man, I just saw the greatest business opportunity. I saw the perfect business."*

What happens when you watch a movie you really like? You can't wait to encourage your coworkers to see it. You can't wait to tell your neighbors. You can't wait to tell your friends, "Man, I saw the greatest movie!" Well, why don't you say, "Man, I just saw the greatest business opportunity. I saw the perfect business."

"What's it all about?" they'd ask.

"Why," you say, "are you interested? It would take me about an hour to explain it. When would be a good time for you?"

Goodness gracious. How hard is that?

---

[*] Amway made $8.8 billion in 2018. Sales have fluctuated in recent years, but stayed strong, never dropping below $8.6 billion as of this writing.

But instead, we're sitting around, worrying about our jobs and the price of gas. Man, if you're worried about the price of gas, you're in trouble. If you're worried about the price of food, I feel sorry for you. But don't worry; do something about it! Don't feel sorry for yourself and your family. Go do something. You don't need that kind of stress! To pick and choose what you can afford to eat and how far you can afford to travel? That's bunk! We don't participate in a recession. Amway does not participate in one. You can grow your business, no matter what the economy is doing.

Here's number nine on Russell's list: The ideal business is relatively free from all kinds of government and industry regulations. You know, OSHA has never showed up on my doorstep. No government regulator has sent me a letter or come to my door to check me out. You know why? Because Amway takes care of all that for us. They have a legal staff that makes sure everything we do complies with the law. They have lobbyists who work with Congress. They do all that for us with top-notch people. They hire the best.

We stack up well on that one. Don't you agree?

Okay, two more. Number ten: The ideal business is portable. You can put it anywhere you want. In Florida, California, the Canary Islands, wherever. That was as big as he could think. We can take it a lot farther. Think about the eighty-five countries and territories we can take our business. All we need is a phone. We can do everything on a smartphone: order products, register people, everything. It's an amazing business, folks.

You've heard people on this stage detail the price we had to pay to get this business to where it is today. Now we're counting on you, the next generation, to take it, stand on our shoulders, and go even further with it. To make it the largest business in the world.

And it's all in place for you to do that, folks. You have a tremendous life ahead of you. Doors are opening, but you must walk through them. If you haven't paid attention to dreaming and you think that's childish, let me remind you that all success starts with a dream. It all starts in your mind, with how you think. Learn to take control of your thought life, to make it work for you. Filter out the negativity. Learn how to think like successful people think. Harness your thoughts to your vision and dreams. Be willing to learn what you don't know and grow. That's what you're doing when you're CORE; you're learning.

Now to the last characteristic, number 11. Here's a crucial but over-looked one. The ideal or perfect business keeps you fascinated. You love it. You fall in love with it. It requires your full intellectual and often your emotional energy.

I guarantee you that this business will do that. We're like John Maxwell in this. Do you think John Maxwell will ever retire? No. Why would he? He's doing what he wants to do. He's doing what brings him joy. Well, that's the way Georgia Lee and I are. I'm as retired as I ever want to be. Retired? What's "retired"? *Retired* to me is getting out from under the control of money and being financially and personally free to make your own choices. That's retirement. I did that at age thirty-five, after three years in the business. Now I'm living for something greater. I'm living so that others can have the same freedom we do.

If Georgia Lee and I can do it, you can do it. You've heard our story. We're nothing special. We're just very, very ordinary people who were in deep trouble in every area of our life, and we were fortunate to have somebody care enough about us to share this business with us—this unique and special business. We didn't know how unique and special it was at first, but I knew one thing: It was something I could do. I could fit that in somewhere in my week.

Why? Because I had a dream big enough to make me want more for my family. That dream caused me to start the process and never quit.

I just stayed consistent through the good times, the bad times, the frustrating times, and the disappointing times. That's life. That's part of any business—and if you're going to go through that anyway, why not do it while building something for yourself and your family? I knew what the rewards were, and I kept after them.

What about you? What's your dream? How far will it take you?

I think it's time to find out.

> 66
>
> *If Georgia Lee and I can do it, you can do it. . . . We're just very, very ordinary people who were in deep trouble in every area of our life, and we were fortunate to have somebody care enough about us to share this business with us.*
>
> 99

Appendix B:
The 10 CORE Habits for Success

These ten work habits are what all of the Diamonds have determined they have in common. None of these habits are required by Amway to be an IBO, nor by World Wide to be a member.

1. **Show the Plan**
    If you want to give your organization a legitimate chance to grow, show the plan to two people (couples or singles) a week. Your goal is to develop a rapport and trust, fully educating the person about this business opportunity.

2. **Personal Use**
    Be loyal to your own store. Change your buying habits, and learn to shop intentionally from yourself. Based on your budget, we will show you how to create a consistent and dependable DITTO® order, to be processed on the first day of each month. This will help you fund your business. Become an expert on the products you sell.

3. **Client Volume**
    Establish *at least* 50 PV of Qualified Customer Volume to start, and build to at least 200 PV by Eagle (see current WWDB parameters for Eagle/Double Eagle) of client volume to be consistent with the Amway™ Customer Volume Rule. Customer volume helps you to be profitable and self-funded.

4. **Be Teachable**

Develop open and honest communication with your actively growing upline mentor. This is your opportunity to access leaders who have built successful businesses. You are encouraged to communicate with your mentor and develop skills on connecting and having conversations.

5. **Audio**

Create a habit of listening to an audio per day. Listening to audios helps you build your belief, enthusiasm, and knowledge.

6. **Read**

Develop a reading habit of at least fifteen minutes per day from the WWDB recommended book list. These books explore subjects like leadership, personal development, and business principles.

7. **Functions**

Successful leaders will provide training and motivation on how to build a successful, profitable business. Prioritize attending local (one each month) and major (four per year) WWDB functions each year.

8. **Be Accountable**

Follow through on the commitment you made to yourself and others. Value the time and knowledge people are willing to give you. Be financially responsible and follow the Cardinal Rules:

   a. Never do anything for the first time without seeking perspective from your mentor.

   b. Never pass negative information to your team or crossline; take all challenges to your mentor.

   c. Never embarrass or put down anyone.

d. Never mess with anyone's money (i.e., investments, loaning, charity, or outside business).

e. Never mess with anyone's spouse.

9. **CommuniKate (unified messaging system)**
As your budget allows, be on CommuniKate. Communi-Kate is the primary form of communication within WWDB. Be inspired, motivated, and trained by leaders. Listen to and clear messages each day. This tool allows you to communicate with your mentor as needed, based on their recommendation.*

10. **Premier Membership**
As your budget allows, maintain a Premier Membership with WWDB. Premier Membership gives you access to business support materials, mobile apps, a connection with your leaders, as well as many other valuable benefits and tools.**

---

* World Wide Group and CommuniKate participation and purchase of the suggested materials is optional and is not a requirement of starting an Amway business. While the techniques and approaches suggested have worked for others, no one can guarantee that these techniques will work for you. We hope, however, that the ideas presented here will assist you in developing a strong and profitable business.

** For IBO use only, not approved for prospects. CR# 96470.

Notes

1. *The Holy Bible: English Standard Version* (Wheaton, IL: Crossway Bibles, 2016), Ecclesiastes 2:13. Scripture quotations taken from *The Holy Bible, English Standard Version*, copyright © 2001 by Crossway Bibles, a division of Good News Publishers, are used by permission. All rights reserved.

2. For a concise summary of this topic, see Carol S. Dweck, Ph.D., "The Power of Yet," YouTube, September 12, 2014, https://www.youtube.com/watch?v=J-swZaKN2Ic&t.

3. Carol S. Dweck, *Mindset* (New York: Random House Publishing group, 2006), loc. 159-162, Kindle. Excerpts from *Mindset: The New Psychology of Success* by Carol S. Dweck, Ph.D., copyright © 2006, 2016, by Carol S. Dweck, Ph.D. Used by permission of Random House, an imprint and division of Penguin Random House LLC. All rights reserved.

4. Ibid., loc. 175-177.

5. Kenneth Nathaniel Taylor, *The Living Bible, Paraphrased* (Wheaton, IL: Tyndale House, 1971, 1997), Mark 9:35. Used by permission of Tyndale House Publishers, Inc., Wheaton, Illinois 60189. All rights reserved.

6. Jim Collins, *Good to Great: Why Some Companies Make the Leap . . . and Others Don't* (New York: HarperBusiness, 2001).

7. See Ephesians 5:22.

8. Zig Ziglar, *See You at the Top* (Gretna, LA: Pelican Publishing, 1977), 205-206. Used by permission of Pelican Publishing. All rights reserved.

9. *The Holy Bible: English Standard Version* (Wheaton, IL: Crossway Bibles, 2016), Romans 13:8.

10. *The Holy Bible: English Standard Version* (Wheaton, IL: Crossway Bibles, 2016), Proverbs 13:22.

11. Helen Steiner Rice, *The Poems and Prayers of Helen Steiner Rice* (Grand Rapids, MI: Fleming H. Revell, 2003), 164. Used with permission of Helen Steiner Rice Foundation Fund, LLC. © 1968 Helen Steiner Rice Foundation Fund, LLC; a wholly owned subsidiary of Cincinnati Museum Center.

12. Jack Hyles, *Blue Denim and Lace*, https://www.baptist-city.com/Books1/Bluedenim.html.

13. Taken from *The Be Happy Attitudes: Eight Positive Attitudes that Can Transform Your Life!* by Robert Schuller, pg. 77. Copyright © 1985, 1996 by Robert H. Schuller. Used by permission of Thomas Nelson. www.thomasnelson.com

14. *The Holy Bible: English Standard Version* (Wheaton, IL: Crossway Bibles, 2016), Matthew 6:21.

15. Excerpt from *Jesus Did It Anyway* by Kent M. Keith, copyright © 2005 by Carlson Keith Corporation. Used by permission of G. P. Putnam's Sons, an imprint of Penguin Publishing Group, a division of Penguin Random House LLC. All rights reserved.

16. *The Holy Bible: English Standard Version* (Wheaton, IL: Crossway Bibles, 2016), James 3:1.

17. *The Holy Bible: Holman Christian Standard Version*. (Nashville: Holman Bible Publishers, 2009), Luke 11:9. Used by Permission HCSB ©1999, 2000, 2002, 2003, 2009 Holman Bible Publishers. Holman Christian Standard Bible®, Holman CSB®, and HCSB® are federally registered trademarks of Holman Bible Publishers.

18. John Mauldin, *Just One Thing: Twelve of the World's Best Investors Reveal the One Strategy You Can't Overlook* (Hoboken, NJ: John Wiley & Sons, Inc., 2006), 209. Used by permission of Wiley & Sons, Inc. All rights reserved.

19. See https://corporatesolutions.johnmaxwell.com/blog/the-5-levels-of-leadership/ and John's books *Developing the Leader Within You* and *The 5 Levels of Leadership*.

GEORGIA LEE PURYEAR, along with her husband, Ron, founded World Wide Dreambuilders in 1979. Starting with nothing other than grit, determination, and a heart for servant leadership, they believed and built a successful Amway business, while teaching others to do what they had learned to do. Today this organization has grown into a community of successful leaders who inspire, educate, and equip more than 73,000 Independent Business Owners across the globe. While remaining very active as a leader, mentor, and speaker, Georgia Lee loves spending time with her family, including eleven grandchildren and four great-grandchildren.

STEPS OF CORE...
...CORE + DO M...

FEW TIPS...
...IN YOUR...
...Y CORE R...
...OR FUNCTI...
...SL...
...LAV ON THE WWDB WEB...
...OR EACH 90 DAY CORE RUN...
...SEND COPY TO YOUR...

...RSELVES TO SET... MOTIVE US... ...THAT OUR FUTURE COULD T... ...ALL AN IMAGINA...
...MOTIVE US TO PROGRESS TOWARDS AND AC...
...TO (MAKE OUR OWN CH...
IT ALSO GAVE US FREE WILL - TO (MAKE OUR OWN CH...
...IT IS EASY TO DO, EASY NOT...
IF YOU STOP AND THINK ABOUT IT, EVERY T...
THAT IS MAN MADE THAT YOU, WAS 1ST JUST A...
...IN SOMEONE'S IMAGINATION.
THAT IS WHY IT'S SO IMPORTANT THAT YOU U...
YOUR IMAGINATION TO DREAM OF WHAT YOU W...
YOUR FUTURE TO LOOK LIKE 1ST. TO WRITE IT D...
TAKE PICTURES OF IT AND PUT IT ON YOUR REFRIG...
OR BATHROOM MIRROR SO YOU SEE IT EVERY DAY.

VISION IS THE DRIVE IN YOUR LIFE. IT...
IS WHAT WILL KEEP YOU DRIVING TOWARDS YOUR
GOAL AND NOT QUIT ON YOURSELF. WITHOUT A
VISION YOU WILL BE MOVED BY A CLOCK (TIME)
    A DREAM WITHOUT ACTION IS A HALLUCINATION.
A DREAM WITH ACTION BECOMES A VISION.
    YOUR DREAMS + GOALS WILL CHANGE AS
YOU PROGRESS TOWARDS YOUR VISION BUT YOUR
VISION + PURPOSE FOR YOUR LIFE WILL REMAIN
THE SAME.
    YOUR DREAMS AND GOALS WILL MOTIVATE,
ENCOURAGE + REWARD YOU AS YOU PURSUE
YOUR LIFE LONG PURPOSE AND VISION FOR YOUR
LIFE.

BUSIN...
1. - WWDB - DEBT FREE - ...
2. - MANAGEMENT TEAM (20 TOP DIAMONDS...
    70% VOTE REQUIRED TO CHANGE OUR CULTURE
3. - APPROVED SYSTEM BY AMWAY CORP. WE NEVE...
    BREAK AMWAY'S RULES, GOD'S LAWS OR M...
    LAWS.
4. - VERTICAL ALIGNMENT - PRIORITIES
    A - GOD - PAUL + BILLIE TSIKA
    B - SPOUSE/CHILDREN

AMWAY - The VEHICLE
WHAT MAKES IT SO SPECIAL?
1- FOUNDED BY 2 CHRISTIAN MEN AND
The SALES + MKTG. PLAN WAS DESIGNED
ON GOD'S LAWS OF SUCCESS - GIVER
BEING A
INSTEAD OF TAKER - LAW OF SOWING
AND REAPING (WILL EXPLAIN TOMORROW AFTERNOON)
(COMPASSIONATE CAPITALISM)

2- PRIVATE CORPORATION - (CONTROL) OF The
MKTG. PLAN - KEEP IT PURE)

3- DEBT FREE (AWESOME POWER IN
COMPETITIVE GLOBAL MARKET) - 45
COUNTRIES + TERRITORYS)

4- 5000 + PRODUCTS + SERVICES - BRAND
NAMES

AND EMOTION - DRIVEN
RACTER - DRIVEN PEOPLE!
DO RIGHT, THEN FEEL GOOD
ARE COMMITMENT DRIVEN
3. MAKE PRINCIPLE - BASED DECISIONS
4. LET ACTION   -ITUDE
5. BELIEVE IT,
6. CREATE MC
7. ASK, "WHA
8. CONTINUE
9. ARE ST
10. ARE LE

THINK IT
JUST ONE
ISCIPLINE + DECIS
FINISH. THAT'S
CHAT DRIVE US

(7)

IGNORANCE (WISEDS)
FAMILY PROBLEMS (HUS + WIFE)
FINANCIAL PROBLEMS (BUDGET)
JOB PROBLEMS
PEOPLE SKILLS

E.D.C.
DIAMOND
EMERALD
RUBY
D.D.

INCOME D
HAR
COR

1YR   2YR   3YR   4Y

A   DREAM → +S VISION
↑   FAITH → B
↑ → CORE → F BELIEF ADDS